WHAT PEOPLE ARE SAYING

Patty is one of those people you'd jump to go anywhere with because she is such incredible fun on the journey. Smart-funny and full of "I-can't-believe-you-actually-did-that" exploits, always topped with large dollops of self-deprecating humor. As she takes you into your overflowing archives of regret or that upstairs closet of secret shame, she opens up her own archives and shines the light of God's truth and love in there (and in yours) so that our failures and rejections lose their ability to paralyze and defeat us. Patty deeply cares about God and people and has a gift for connecting the two with Biblical truth about forgiveness, grace, and what it really means to be a new creation, loved by God more than we can imagine.

LAEL ARRINGTON, Author & Speaker

If you like to laugh out loud and be inspired at the same time, read this book. Patty LaRoche's written words are hilariously funny, gut-level honest, heart-wrenchingly transparent, and filled with practical take-aways and truths from God's Word that will change your life for the better. You'll find this book entertaining, enriching, and uplifting. *A Little Faith Lift* is the perfect gift for any occasion.

CAROL KENT, Speaker & Author
He Holds My Hand: Experiencing God's Presence & Protection (Tyndale)

I met Patty LaRoche through her boys, which makes me love her and this book even more. She unashamedly, and often hilariously, strips her life down to the bare bones to reveal the deep truths that God has taught her along the way. Through laughter and tears you will be reminded how much you are loved by God, just the way we are. I can't think of anything better than that!

KORIE ROBERTSON
Duck Dynasty, Strong and Kind

A LITTLE FAITH LIFT . . . FINDING JOY BEYOND REJECTION

Patty LaRoche

Carpenter's Son Publishing

A Little Faith Lift: Finding Joy Beyond Rejection
©2023 Patty LaRoche

Scripture taken from THE HOLY BIBLE, NEW INTERNATIONAL VERSION®, NIV®
Copyright © 1973, 1978, 1984, 2011 by Biblica, Inc.™ Used by permission.
All rights reserved worldwide.

Published by Carpenter's Son Publishing, Franklin, Tennessee

Edited by Bob Irvin

Front cover illustration by Pamela Nielsen

Cover and Interior Design by Suzanne Lawing

Interior graphics by Montana LaRoche

Printed in the United States of America

978-1-954437-83-8

DEDICATION

Over the years it has taken me to finish *A Little Faith Lift*, many people have come alongside me, offering encouragement. Lael Arrington, on numerous occasions, patiently walked me through the ever-changing, social media requirements, pretending not to hear me when I groaned, "I just don't get it." Her connections were life-changing, as she introduced me to Carol Kent's "Speak Up with Confidence" ministries, asked me to lead her church Bible study and never rolled her eyes when I needed help tweaking a sentence or two…or ten. Friends like Robin, Brian, Marti, Sally, Elaine, Pam, Howard, Frank and Juliette, my perpetual cheerleaders, refused to give up on me when I answered their "How's your book coming?" with "It's not. I'm a failure."

Encouragement came also through people who permitted me to include their zany stories in *A Little Faith Lift* and told me they laughed until they cried. John and Chrys Howard believed in my book. They also warned me that publishers look for a sizeable social media following, something which required extra effort on my part. John was relentless and introduced me to Shane at Christian Book Services who believed in my writing and started me on the road to turning my stories of rejection into an actual book with real pages and end notes. Hallelujah!

Bob Irvin, my editor, was incredible and poured over *A Little Faith Lift*'s contents, making suggestions and improvements and telling me that I'm "funny with a much-needed message." Thank you for your expertise and believing in me, Bob.

Then there are my adult children and their spouses who constantly asked how my book was coming and offered to join Instagram to get my numbers up. Thanks to them, I quickly increased my followers to, oh, say, twenty. My granddaughter, Mo, who designed the chapter sketches, eyed them much more critically than I and was relentless, making sure her images met my approval. Pam, my artist friend who knows me well, created my book cover from her magical heart collection.

Dave, my husband, has been the stalwart behind this undertaking. He never asked, "Are you really going to finish this book?" (which had to cross his mind a kajillion times) but instead, celebrated when I received encouraging news and told me that he was sorry when publishers rejected my book because of that social media thing.

The real credit, however, goes to God for teaching me that Rejection (real or imaginary) does not devalue me and for giving me plenty of anecdotes to use in this book. He created me with the ability to laugh at myself and to see value in others. I pray *A Little Faith Lift* gives Him the glory He deserves.

CONTENTS

introduction 11

one   FAN TANGLE, ANYONE?. 13

two   PUBERTY, MEET PUT-DOWNS 23

three   JUDGING THE JUDGE. 31

four   ROUND AND ROUND WE GO 37

five   WILL THE GOOD SAMARITAN
           PLEASE STAND UP? 49

six   A LESSON FROM THE
           ACADEMY AWARDS 63

seven   OUT ON A LIMB . . .
           AND NOT IN A FUN WAY 71

eight   A WASTE OF TASTE 81

nine   PAYBACK 93

ten   FIRST, LAST . . . LAST, FIRST 101

eleven SEW WHAT?. 113

twelve THE DISEASE TO PLEASE 127

thirteen DISHONORABLE INTENTIONS 137

fourteen THE PITFALLS OF LEADERSHIP 143

fifteen AT WHAT POINT? 153

sixteen SAY YES TO FEAR? SAY NO TO JOY 165

seventeen	IT'S MY PITY PARTY AND I'LL CRY IF I WANT TO. 173
eighteen	MAYBE LOOKS CAN KILL 185
nineteen	THE WORST FAILURE? FAILING TO TRY. . . 199
twenty	THE SHAME OF SHAME 211
twenty-one	KINDERGARTEN CHAOS. 221
twenty-two	GOIN' DOWN 229
twenty-three	WHEN THE NEEDLE SAYS 'EMPTY' 239
twenty-four	TAKE AWAY THE ENEMY'S POWER: FORGIVE 247
twenty-five	SO, WHAT'S A PERSON TO DO? 255
Endnotes	 261
About the Author	 265

INTRODUCTION

I would love to write that I have the utmost confidence in the success of *A Little Faith Lift...Finding Joy Beyond Rejection*. That you readers will read it, laugh until you cry, cry until you laugh, submit five-star reviews on it, buy hundreds of copies and follow me on Instagram. Yes, I would love to write that, but honestly, I fear the very thing about which this book is written—Rejection.

What if I can't take my own advice and let God be the only audience that counts? What if I can't find humor in someone saying I'm not funny, even though that is the one trait that has gotten me through a multitude of demeaning situations? What if?

For over fifty years, I have been involved with my husband and sons in the world of professional baseball, a world which only exacerbated my insecurities. An altercation with a center fielder's wife allowed me to realize God had not created me to be devalued. Instead, He grieved every time I gave someone else permission to define me.

I have feared rejection much of my life and needed a faith-lift when it came to representing the Lord consistently. I had mastered the Christian "look," smiling on the outside while groaning on the inside, but I was exhausted from the charade, from phony Christian platitudes that masked a death squad of judgmental, critical thoughts.

I would read that Jesus' sheep knew His voice and questioned if I belonged to someone else's flock. And Heaven forbid if a burning bush were to appear in my living room—I would have grabbed my fire extinguisher and blasted away. I knew about God but not God.

As I finalize this book, my son, Adam, has been to Ukraine five times to help with the rescue of orphans and widows. Listening to him, I understand that my humorous experiences with rejection don't come close to what the Ukrainians have endured, nor do they compare with others I know who have dealt with painful divorces or sex slavery or ritual abuse. What I do know is that we all are loved by a merciful, compassionate, loving Father who longs to help our relationship with Him come alive.

A Little Faith Lift…Finding Joy Beyond Rejection focuses on how we must reject rejection, and even though I am confident this book is life-changing, even though I know that the stories inside these pages expose a multitude of ways in which people—including me—have been told that they aren't good enough, I have met many senior citizens who rue the years they spent comparing themselves to others; sadly, some take that lament to their graves.

It doesn't have to be that way. All we have to do is recognize Satan's devious handiwork when he attempts to weave it into our God-created fabric and trust that no one roots for us, cherishes us, loves us like our Heavenly Father does.

And dear reader, if you take nothing else from *A Little Faith Lift…Finding Joy Beyond Rejection*, please, please remember this: He is the audience that counts.

one

FAN TANGLE, ANYONE?

Be yourself. Everyone else is taken.
OSCAR WILDE

Much of my life has been poured out on the altar of trying to measure up, sacrificing my self-worth to gain the elusive approval of others. Whether because red, frizzy hair, freckles, and spindly legs were easy targets, or because the nuns in my Catholic school secretly conjured up ways to torture me (branding my desire to fit in as "willful disobedience"), or because my widowed mother could not afford a car or a television set, it would be nearly a lifetime before I could erase the damage of those early years.

Not even marrying into—and spending most of my years in—the hyper-competitiveness of the professional baseball world could erase the insecurity. In fact, the pressure of a bigger platform in which the spotlight grew brighter only heightened my hurt, especially when I became known as "the baseball wife who tangled with a fan and lost."

I mean, to be mortified is one thing. To be mortified in front of the entire New York Yankees organization—when you're married to one of its players—is another.

It was 1981, and the Yankees were playing the Oakland A's in the American League playoffs. George Steinbrenner, the Yankees' owner, had chartered two jumbo jets for the players and their wives to make the trip to California for the third game of the series.

Dave, my husband, at thirty-one nearing the end of his twelve-year big league career, and yet pitching well, was keenly aware his baseball years were winding down. We and our two young sons lived in the suburbs with our dear friends, Frank and Janet. Most of the other players and their wives lived in Manhattan. When their husbands were away on road trips, the young wives shopped, attended Broadway plays, and hung out at each other's apartments. I must admit that sometimes I felt minor—all right, *major*—insecurity pangs as the wives would discuss their city exploits, and I had not been included.

Hard to believe, but that was forty years ago.

I'm over that now.

Sort of.

One evening, sitting in Yankee Stadium a few days before postseason play began, the wives resumed a topic that had dominated recent conversations: what they would wear to the baseball playoffs, a discussion that revealed a huge disparity in how we would look. I owned no fur coats, diamond bracelets, one-karat earrings, or designer shoes.

I did, however, have a nice cream-colored suit that miraculously had emerged unscathed from baby throw-up and hot dog mustard stains. This was critical. Every spouse understood the protocol of the playoffs and World Series. The television cameras periodically panned the "wives' section" while the announcer told the entire world who was appearing onscreen. Sort of like the Baseball Oscars . . . minus the red carpet and Versace gowns. Then again, with a couple of these wives, there was always that possibility.

I had to look perfect.

My dear friend Kathy, a roommate from my stewardess days, and I had made arrangements to meet at the Oakland hotel to head to the game together. After deplaning and busing it across town, I had just enough time to reapply deodorant and curl my hair—no easy task since it went halfway down my back. As rare as it was, on this day I felt pretty.

Mr. Steinbrenner generously had chartered a bus for the stockholders, the Yankees players who were on the disabled list, and the spouses. My friend and I waited for the other wives to board. Not because I was nice. Because that's what insecure people do when they want to be liked.

Finally boarding, and stepping on just ahead of Kathy, I turned to comment on how crowded the bus was. I think I managed to get out the words "This bus is . . . " before I began to smell smoke. Was it possible our bus was on fire? Immediately Kathy began screaming. I turned to run off the bus . . . but couldn't. The nauseating stench of burning hair indicated the bus wasn't on fire—I was!

My hair was being sucked into the blades of the dashboard fan.

Pulling me steadily into a backbend position, within milliseconds my once-long tresses were completely entangled in the metal blades, all while the bus driver sat (wide-eyed and body frozen) in his seat, too paralyzed to push his whirlybird's off button. Finally, the motor, realizing it won the battle, surrendered.

After a hotel maintenance worker spent thirty minutes disassembling the metal pinwheel monster, I was freed. Slithering to the rear of the bus, my face a shade of red typically reserved for sun-dried tomatoes, my body resembled a U-turn. I envisioned a future walking hunched over backwards in which I would dress upside down and eat off the floor.

Bucky Dent, the famous Yankees shortstop, who was on the disabled list, was the only one to make eye contact. The rest of the Yankees entourage was faking enthrallment with the palm trees outside the bus windows. Once we arrived at the Oakland Coliseum, Kathy and I got our game passes and then bolted to the nearest restroom where I had my first look at my hair.

My hair! Its fan-fried ends, now chopped off at my shoulders, resembled a collection of Fourth of July, burnt-out sparklers. Repairing the damage was like styling the hair on one of those rubber dolls— you know, the ones with heads punctuated with pea-sized holes, each having one solo strand of hair protruding from it.

Surely no cameraman would be so insensitive as to pick me out of the crowd. I could just see it: "Joe DiMaggio reporting. And here we have the Yankees wives' section where we see a group of beautiful . . . OH NO, WAIT! What's with the woman with the red alfalfa sprouts on her head? Maybe we should call security!"

I turned to the Lord. All I asked was to find my ballpark seat as inconspicuously as possible, slouch to ground level, and stay there until my hair grew out.

Silly me. I forgot that God has a sense of humor, especially when I was involved, and this was His Comedy Central moment.

It seems that Mr. Bucky Dent couldn't wait to share my humiliation with his teammates because, about that time, heads popped out of the dugout with Dave, my husband, in the middle of the sadistic pack. The entire roster of players scanned our section to get a peek at the freak sitting in the wives' section. Had I been carrying one of those "whack-a-mole" mallets, I would have conked an entire team of hysterical New York Yankees. The truth is, if there is one cell in my brain to remind me of any delight I took from that day, I cannot recall it.

Fast-forward twenty-five years. My husband, now coaching in the Yankees' minor leagues, was in spring training in Florida. With our three sons in high school, I had managed to get away to join him for a weekend. It was the first game I had attended that spring, so imagine my surprise when, upon entering the stands, Willie Randolph's wife, Gretchen, yelled my name. Gracious sakes alive! I hadn't seen her since our husbands played together on the Yankees, and I had forgotten that her husband was now the manager of this Yankees team. Gretchen stood, enthusiastically turned to the other, much younger, wives, pointed at me, and said, "There she is. There she is! That's her. That's Patty LaRoche. That's the one who caught her hair in the fan!"

This was not the way I had intended the life of a major league baseball player's wife to pan out. Certainly not what I envisioned as a twelve-year-old.

She, this gorgeous, poised creature, was reclining across the pool from me. I, a spindly almost-teen—an *unimportant*, spindly almost-teen—found myself gawking at her, fantasizing what it would be like to be so famous. My friend had invited me to Kansas City to swim at the pool where her cousin was a member, and there was Anita Piniella, wife of baseball player Lou, lounging at the shallow end.

It was the closest I had ever been to a real celebrity, and I was spellbound. To me, she was exquisite. But, of course, being an athlete's wife would guarantee that . . . wouldn't it?

Little did I know that, twelve years later, I would be entering that same world where I would be reminded that, as glamorous as it looked, even being married to a professional baseball player and living a lifestyle in the spotlight couldn't change me from the outside in.

It should at least have helped. After all, even trips to the grocery store validated my importance, didn't they? Clerks would recognize my last name and ask if I was "the" Mrs. LaRoche. Those in line would crane their necks for a look/see and whisper, and suddenly even they would start murmuring. We were asked to be involved in charities and celebrity fashion shows in the off-season. I was finally somebody. Important.

At least it appeared that way to a lot of other people.

Which, in my then-world, was the only thing that mattered. (And yes, "superficial" and "pitiful" are appropriate synonyms for my yearnings.)

The question *Am I good enough?* has plagued both Christian and non-Christian alike. Interesting, isn't it? Once we buy into the lie that we are inadequate, no amount of trophies or positions are enough to fill the void. We wake up each morning with our "if onlys" revved and rolling. "If only Ryan would notice me." "If only I could lose ten pounds." "If only I could be a starter on the team." "If only I could move up the corporate ladder." "If only *you fill in the blank*." And please hear me here, if you hear nothing else. Anytime you attach an "if only" to your adequacy, you are on a path of inadequacy.

> Once we buy into the lie that we are inadequate, no amount of trophies or positions are enough to fill the void.

I don't know about you, but I gave far too much power to the conflicting recordings circulating in my head. On my exceptional days, like when my hair stylist had done her magic, or the bathroom scales dipped a couple of ounces, or someone complimented my lipstick, my nice soundtrack whispered, "I am okay." That used to happen, oh, about .0000001 percent of the time. The rest of the time my nasty, self-defeating recording bellowed, "If only . . . "

I don't think I'm alone. Who of us doesn't have bouts of insignificance? Who of us doesn't pull out the scales and weigh our giftedness against others, even in Christian circles, where we base our worth on how we compare to others more gifted than ourselves?

If your life is like mine, a mixed bag of disappointments and accomplishments, unless you have a complete change in your belief system, one constant will remain: the pain of not measuring up will rob you of your joy and the satisfaction that could be gained from your greatest successes and the lessons learned from your failures. You will find yourself on an emotional roller coaster, depending on the message you have been given that moment, and one, at that, delivered by other created, sinful beings. You will live in a world of pretending. Pretending to be someone you are not. Hoping your lack of confidence is not found out.

I look back, years later, on my hair-in-the-fan incident and realize that most secure people would have laughed it off. And, possibly, had it been an isolated incident, I too would have found its humor. But for me, much of my life, no matter what role I played, seemed like a collage of inadequacy.

I grieve now over the number of years I spent with that mindset.

My prayer is that you do not do the same.

If you're with me, I want to encourage you to find a comfortable chair and get prepared to spend some time in the pages ahead where we will expose the enemy's tactics to render us broken in our false sense of inadequacy. We will learn that, without intervention, our mind effortlessly morphs into his playground, one in which a daily teeter-totter ride of a compliment, an A+ grade, a positive evaluation, or a closed sale quickly sinks under Satan's reminders of how *un*pretty, *un*popular, *un*fun, *un*creative, *un*skinny, *un*talented, *un*respected . . . *un*whatever we are.

Oh, people, we are missing God's grand adventure for our lives.

We forget that that is not how we were designed. We were not born that way.

> Much of my life, no matter what role I played, seemed like a collage of inadequacy.

Fresh from the womb, we squall and demand and think we're pretty important stuff, but once the world has its way, too many of us take our shattered psyches to the grave without ever giving God—who sees us as complete, loved, and forgiven—permission to be the spiritual glue designed to repair our jagged edges.

If you, like the majority of people I meet, struggle with being "enough," if you stress over making conversation at a company social or discovering that a neighbor hosted a gathering that didn't include you, if the three thousand hand-glittered icicles you created for the church Christmas pageant went unnoticed, or even if standing up for handshake time during church is an effort, this book is for you. And if you are tired of the enemy's mastery at making you feel inadequate, causing you to contrast yourself with others who have the looks, talents, power, or personality traits you don't, this book is for you.

Or perhaps this isn't as much for you as it is for your children. If you, like so many people I meet, are desperate to teach them how to defeat Satan in his game of "Anything you can do, someone else can do better," *A Little Faith Lift* will give you tools to communicate how they, like you, are valued because they are God's masterpiece. How they, like you, are created in His image. How they, like you, are more than adequate. How they, like you, are loved unconditionally by the One who matters most.

But before diving too deeply into these pages, let me be clear what this book is not. It is not about serious, psychological matters—such as sexual abuse—that are of such a sober nature that no humor can be, nor should be, found in them. Comparing those events with teenagers feeling inadequate because of a classroom bully or knobby knees or a nose zit would be foolhardy at best. After recently meeting with a rescued human-trafficking victim who was in hiding until a safe place could be found, I realize the trauma from her experience is far more than I ever will be capable of understanding.

A Little Faith Lift also is not a quick-fix, wake-up-in-the-morning-and-be-epically-confident,   ten-step-program-to-understand-your-value-in-Christ, one-size-fits-all book of suggestions.

I should be so smart.

In these pages I welcome you into my world, where too much of my life was a yardstick with which I measured everything I did and said against someone who did or said it better. From childhood to stewardess to wife, mother, stepmother and grandmother, nothing—not even life in the professional baseball world—was enough to counter my feelings of inadequacy.

Fortunately, God continues to change me. Heal my wounded heart. Sometimes He even used the hurts of others to show me the obvious. As a high school teacher/coach/director, I saw, on a daily basis, the desperation of the teenage competition contest at work, and I longed to gather those students under my spiritual wings and show them what God had done for me.

So when some of those teens asked if I would lead a Bible study for them, I was thrilled. Our weekly discussions—woven into this book, and offered in present tense as I tell the accounts here—opened my eyes to the stranglehold Satan had on their precious lives. I did not want my journey of inadequacy to be theirs.

Nor do I want it be yours.

So please, settle in. Prepare to laugh with me at some of my crazy, embarrassing experiences that helped put my self-esteem on life support. Prepare to . . .

- delve into the destructive thought processes designed to keep you on the pity pot and learn how to squash those merciless, self-defeating beliefs;

- recognize the skewed lines of Satan, who convinces you to use others' opinions of you to determine your value;

- be transparent with God about the fears that have left you unenthused about taking risks as you recognize who is behind your 'fraidy-cat traps;

- fall more deeply in love with your heavenly Father, and with a renewed passion, as you begin to understand how valued you are;

- accept that everything in this world has the potential to pull us from God in spite of how He is up to something epic in each of our lives;

- celebrate your new beginning as you find joy and share it with others.

More importantly, join me as I share with you how God continually steps in to redeem my experiences and encourages me to see myself as He sees me.

Just as He wants to do for you.

two

PUBERTY, MEET PUT-DOWNS

I want to be the best version of myself.
JERSHIKA MAPLE, ON *THE VOICE*, 2021

Rejection is not something I want to think about much, but if you're like the other 99.9 percent of people on this planet, you have given someone or something the power to make you feel less than God intended. You understand the uncompromising pain of being the bull's-eye for verbal and emotional arrows slung from the compound bows of relatives, teachers, coaches, friends, coworkers, or even strangers. The quote at the top of this chapter screams a message we all need to remember.

The high school students I taught all had stories of being targeted. One assignment on self-concept was proof.

In my speech class, students were to write five adjective-noun combinations that described them. Typically, most were negative (unkind brother, rotten troublemaker, stupid student, unorganized procrastinator, uncoordinated athlete, and so on). Beside each description they explained what or who made them accept that label. Parents were the main culprits. But classmates ran a close second.

Predominantly middle schoolers. Apparently, that is where puberty and put-downs become pals.

After all, if a thirteen-year-old can squash whatever self-worth a classmate has managed to salvage up to that point, she claws a few more rungs up the status ladder. So if the hormonal roller coaster ride, the acne breakouts, the gangly legs and arms, and the hair emerging from previously bald areas aren't enough to make one feel a little despairing, classmates are there to help.

This assignment from my students proved it, and based on my teaching experience, this had become an all-too-familiar story.

I was in my fifth year as the high school forensics coach when a group of my female students decided I needed to host a slumber party at my house. Dave had left for spring training, our sons were grown and gone, and these girls just knew that I was "lonely and needed company." I assured them I definitely was *not* lonely and that I had a very full, active life, and as much as I enjoyed being around them, I would survive quite nicely without their companionship, thank you very much.

They knew otherwise and scheduled a sleepover for the following Friday night.

When that evening arrived, my living room was transformed into a camp dormitory with sleeping bags, makeup totes, six-packs of Diet Coke, several bags of potato chips, and a dozen giddy high school girls wearing furry house slippers and flannel pajamas. They lacked for no shortage of entertainment. From make-overs to charades to improv acting competitions to a dance competition, they were in high gear. And when their activities finally wore down in the wee hours of the morning, their mouths did not; they began comparing middle school experiences. Most had stories of rejection and hurt, and surprisingly, the majority admitted bouncing on both sides of the put-down teeter-totter.

Maureen related a hurtful tale that happened in seventh grade soon after she had moved to Fort Scott, Kansas, home of our local school district. Most of her thirteen-year-old classmates had shunned her, and she didn't know why. One day she wore the exact outfit that a popular girl wore. When the two look-alikes were near each other in the hallway, the "in" crowd made a point of complimenting their friend and then turned to Maureen to tell her how ugly she looked in her clothes. Now, mind you, I knew Maureen as a beautiful, talented, fun, high school student. The year of our sleepover, she was captain of the dance team and had several close friends. Ironically, some of those same gal-pals had been involved in the middle school abuse.

Following Maureen's anecdote, the verbal barn doors opened, and each girl had a turn to tell her story. Several described the hierarchy of their particular clique by explaining that one girl "ruled," and each week her clan would select one of its members to be on the "outs." The alienated teen was forbidden to eat with her friends or stand near them. She was fodder for their cruel comments until her time under their sentence was up. Then, one week later, she would be back "in" their sweet little graces and someone else would be excluded.

Saturday Night Live actress Amy Poehler wrote about a similar experience in teenage rejection. "Almost every girl goes through this weird living nightmare, where you show up at school and realize people have grown to hate you overnight. It's a *Twilight Zone* moment when you can't figure out what is real. . . . There should be manuals passed out to teach girls how to handle that inevitable one-week stretch when up is down and the best friend who just slept over at your house suddenly pulls your hair in front of everyone and laughs."[1]

Sadly, this behavior continues.

Rejection is huge for, but not limited to, teenage girls.

In April 2022, a public relations nightmare unfolded in the White House. Barack Obama, the U.S. President for two terms that preceded the presidency of Joe Biden by four years, was invited to speak to a group of select Democrats applauding the tenth anniversary of ObamaCare, the universal health care program passed into law under Obama's tutelage.

Following the charismatic Obama's talk, those in attendance encircled him, fawning over the opportunity to be near their political hero. The cameras caught a rejection tragedy unfolding, for President Biden looked like a lost soul, struggling to find someone to pay attention to him. Biden meandered on the outskirts of the celebratory Obama swarm, his loneliness reminding me of middle schoolers sitting by themselves at a cafeteria table, desperate to be noticed. The airways played the tape ad nauseum. Let me clarify that I am not a Biden fan. I do, however, respect the position of President and can only imagine what those few moments of feeling like a "nobody" had to be like.

A week later, someone sent out a musical version of Biden's humiliation. "All By Myself" played in the background as we viewed Biden trying to get Obama's attention, only to finally give up, wander aimlessly in the background, and ultimately reach for the hand of some woman in the audience. Here he was, the president of the most powerful nation in the world, and his humiliation was being compounded for others to mock.

Then I realized something. If Jesus wasn't above rejection, why should any human, no matter how powerful, be different? Of course, Jesus didn't have some background music track accompanying His torturous death, but he did have Roman guards competing for His clothing and mocking His pain. More tragically, on the cross He endured the ultimate rejection. Matthew 27:45 tells us that at the ninth hour Jesus cried out, "My God, my God, why hast thou forsaken me?" God Himself turned His back on the sins of the world—our sins!—for whom Christ was giving up His life.

Could there ever be a greater rejection? I think not.

The girls at my slumber party all had their personal stories of rejection. As rankled as I was upon hearing Maureen's story, I was more saddened as I watched these girls shed not a few tears when they recalled the pain and embarrassment of their role as both victims and perpetrators of this cruel middle school game. Yes, perpetrators. They shared that there was a certain power that accompanied their controlling behavior, and as long as they were dishing out the trash talk, they were in command, enjoying their merciless role and breathing a sigh of thankful relief that they were not the bullies' target.

Years later, after that group graduated, I was able to use their examples in my communications class when we addressed the power of words. Everyone had a story, but Jessie, one of the juniors, shared an incident I found particularly troublesome. It happened the week before on the school bus between a twelve-year old and a six-year-old. Jessie overheard the pre-teen repeatedly picking on the youngster, calling her "fat" and "ugly." Jessie intervened and confronted the middle schooler, asking how *she* would like to be made fun of.

That night the bully's mother phoned Jessie, called her names (not suitable for a Christian book), and reminded her that there is "such a thing as freedom of speech" and that her daughter "said nothing but the truth—that first-grader was fat and ugly." Wow! I was livid and shared with Jessie that the wormy apple certainly didn't fall far from the diseased tree.

Naturally, she had no idea how a piece of fruit related to her bus story.

The point is, there always will be someone who sees us as undesirable and flawed. Our Maker knows differently. Each cell in our body boasts His stamp of approval, and our distinctions are part of His grand design. We are God's best. Those who choose to laugh at, mock, or bully others ignore how hurtful their behaviors are to their victims. And to God.

> There always will be someone who sees us as undesirable and flawed. Our Maker knows differently. Each cell in our body boasts His stamp of approval, and our distinctions are part of His grand design. We are God's best.

When my grandson Drake was in sixth grade, he regularly encountered a hefty eighth-grader who liked to poke fun at him. When Drake shared these confrontations with me, I, like most loving grandparents I know, threatened to take matters into my own strangling hands. Drake said that he didn't mind being targeted because the kid was "really funny."

"But Drake," I countered, "bullying is not funny, and this kid is a big-time bully."

"Yeah, but he's really funny. So I just laugh at him and tell him he's really funny and he gets upset and leaves."

Personally, I found that odd and still wanted to meet that punk alone in a dark alley.

To pray with him, of course.

After I choked him.

Most victims don't react to these put-downs the way my grandson did. Should they report their abuse to an administrator or parent to complain, the tormentor's repercussions can be terrifying. As a teacher, I made a point of talking about what my students should do if they were bullied or if they witnessed bullying. Verbal paybacks or remaining silent were not in my array of suggestions. I counseled that the best solution was to confront the bully directly. "May I ask what thrill you get in trying to make me feel bad about myself?" or "May I ask what thrill you get in trying to make _____ feel bad about him/herself?" I told them that they probably should not anticipate an apology—probably more like a punch in the gut—but needed to press for an answer and not back down.

During my teaching days, once between classes, I witnessed a towering freshman picking on a smaller classmate at the end of my hall. The larger one was smacking the defenseless one, first on one side of his head and then the other. The victim was cowering, laughing out of embarrassment, shielding his head with his hands while classmates looked on.

As one who had preached against bullying, one who knows that a tough guy acts that way for a reason and needs a little guidance to behave with more kindness, I had an opportunity to turn two young men's lives around.

Too bad that never entered my mind. Neither teen saw me coming, but come I did, thankful that God gave me hands large enough to spread two keys past an octave on the piano. Grabbing Bully Boy by the back of his neck, I spun him around to face me, nose to nose. And went bonkers.

"You think that's funny, slapping someone around because he's not able to defend himself? Well, let me tell you how things work in my hallway, punk. You and I are going to the office, and if I ever again see you do anything remotely close to what I just witnessed, I'll be tickled pink to call for an administrator—who happens to be several inches taller than you—to smack you around in the same way you just smacked your classmate. *Are we clear?*" Only because I was imprinting teeth marks on my tongue did I not continue my tirade.

And yes, I realized no administrator was going to hit a student (side note: sometimes I miss those days), and yes, I realize that my anger did not represent Christlikeness.

But . . . whatever.

I mean, let's not forget there is that little table-turning incident in the temple.[2] It is probably one of my favorite Scripture passages in the entire Bible.

Even today, with all the public campaigns centered around anti-bullying efforts, stories abound. This week I connected with Dwayne, a former Seattle policeman, who shared a story with me. On duty, he received a call from a mother whose daughter was being text-bullied from, of all places, a group of girls attending a Bible study.

Say what?? Christians, Christians! How are we failing so badly?

Perhaps you have your own hair-raising memories of being victimized, of being picked on, of feeling like you owed the world an apology for merely existing. Chances are you even remember the details: the taunting expressions, the exact words, what your tormentor was wearing. And whenever you think of how you were treated, you vow to never again give anyone that kind of power.

I pray you don't. I pray that as you read the following chapters, you learn how valued you are and determine to realize that you have the power to control your own destiny.

Because, with God's help, you can.

three

JUDGING THE JUDGE

<u>Sometimes I Want</u>
Sometimes I want to put a gun to my head and pop it.
Sometimes I want to visit that place in the sky.
Sometimes I want to say goodbye to the world and fly to the sky.
Sometimes I want to be six feet underground with the worms.
Sometimes I want to leave this world
And today is one of those days.

This poem, written in my theater class by one of my high school juniors, was submitted as an example of word repetition. It was certainly not what I expected.

The last year before I retire from teaching, one of my high school students comes to me and asks if I will lead a Bible study for her and six of her friends who are struggling with typical teenage issues and want a deeper walk with the Lord. I was aware that Dara, our school secretary, recently led a Bible study that concentrated on a young woman's inner, versus outer, beauty. Perfect. I order the study guides and borrow her leader's packet. I am going to impart pearls of wisdom to change their lives for the better. I tell myself I can do this.

The eight of us meet weekly. I make tacos for the group and then we curl up in my living room and get to work. It takes little time to realize they are a lot like me . . . okay, like me except for little things like skin tone, bodies the size of drinking straws, hair—yes, plentiful hair—wrinkleless faces, athleticism, beauty, intelligence, talent, and popularity. At least that's how I see them. As it turns out, they see themselves quite differently. These girls eat rejection for lunch. Our first Bible study proves that.

Some have "looked for love in all the wrong places"; others have relied on starvation diets, popularity contests, faddish clothes, self-mutilation, and even cocaine to make themselves feel accepted. And here they are, sharing their pain, rejection, and realization that the externals cannot fix what is happening on the inside.

To hear them talk, they will be validated once they find their Prince Charming and start raising a family. That, of course, won't happen until they are prettier, more popular, and more talented. It is obvious they have tied their identity to temporal things, things they surely realize can easily be lost. With their wounded words, my teenage years flash before my eyes, for I too had the same misconceptions at their age.

Now I know differently. Not a day goes by that I allow my feelings of inadequacy to alter the way I think or behave.

Okay, that's not entirely true, but I cannot dismiss the truth that I am far better off than I was for much of my life.

For these high school girls, their "truths" are lies. There is no perfect man, no matter how many weights he bench presses or how many times he brings you roses. Child-raising is the most ridiculously difficult profession ever imagined, and if you have kids like mine, you will sometimes go to bed begging for the Rapture to come. If these teens want to snatch a guy based on their looks, what will happen when they get to be my age and their eighteen-inch waist bloats into an inner tube circling their gut, beneficial only should they need to save their lives after falling off an all-you-can-eat buffet cruise ship?

I need wisdom. I fear these wonderful young women might settle for a life of wishing—not for what could have been but for what should have been. Listening to them, I think to myself: *What might I say to encourage these girls not to give their circumstances (or significant others) the power to destroy the view God has of them?* Especially since it is a battle in which I have spent much of my life on the front lines.

My immediate response is to point out their individual attributes, their accomplishments, and tell them how treasured they are to God, but my comments are as productive as a screen door on a submarine. They have bought into their negative self-perception for so long that my paltry, two-minute compliments will not possibly erase the years of damage.

Instead, they choose to believe Satan's lies as he daily finds ways to remind them of their inadequacy. If they truly are inferior, then God made a mistake when He created them. It is no wonder their desire to take risks and move forward to glorify God is a struggle. They don't recognize it as that, but by rejecting how the Potter has molded their "clay,"[3] that inference can be made.

So what happens now? Unless they change that poisoned mindset, they will morph into chameleons, wear masks to please others, and, in the process, fail to understand who they were designed to be.

In other words, make the same choices I did for far too long.

"And if you're the ones most admired in our school, can you imagine how others feel?" I ask them. "No doubt, the others in the hallway have the same view of themselves. They might fake competence like you do, but has it occurred to you that they would love to have your looks or your talents or your brains or your morals or your personality or your home life or even to be a part of a Bible study like this? If all of you think of yourselves so critically, and you're the ones most looked up to in our school, can you imagine what they're thinking? Probably the same, if not worse, than you."

🏆 🏆 🏆

The irony is obvious. These girls wonder how they are being judged while their judges no doubt think the same. And as long as they buy into another person's criticism of them, real or imagined, they will rely on someone whose perspective is as distorted as theirs. This is no minor issue. According to Mitch Prinstein, a University of North Carolina psychologist, "When we're reliant on others for our sense of self, only feeling good if we get positive feedback or markers of status, we're at risk for depression."[4]

Serious stuff.

Most of us are no different than these girls. We give ourselves permission to feel deficient when someone or something (again, real or imaginary) makes us feel inferior, and Heaven help us if we ever do anything embarrassing in front of a group of people—the earth might as well just swallow us up right there because we're never going out in public again. (Trust me, I know.) I address the girls sitting in my living room with that exact issue.

> These girls wonder how they are being judged while their judges no doubt think the same. And as long as they buy into another person's criticism of them, real or imagined, they will rely on someone whose perspective is as distorted as theirs.

Are you with me here? Can you see the futility in such thinking? Hopefully at this point you are cheering for these young women to get it together, to not give their eternal enemy any ammunition, and to give God a chance, right? Awesome.

I want the same for you, but first we have to recognize that our deficiencies just might be our greatest strengths. I love the story of the Chinese water bearer who had two large pots, each hanging on the ends of a pole he carried across his neck. One of the pots had a crack in it, while the other pot was perfect and always delivered a full jar of water. For two years, at the end of the long walk from the stream to the house, the cracked pot arrived only half full. One day the poor, ashamed, cracked pot spoke to the water bearer. "I'm ashamed of myself because this crack in my side causes water to leak out all the way back to your house."

The bearer answered, "Did you notice that there are flowers only on your side of the path, but not on the other pot's side? That's because I have always known about your flaw, and I planted flower seeds on your side of the path, and every day while we walk back, you've watered them. For two years I have been able to pick these beautiful flowers to decorate the table. Without you, there would not be this beauty to grace the house."

Moral: Each of us should be satisfied being a cracked pot.

🏆   🏆   🏆

As we close our first meeting in prayer, these special young ladies seem comforted to know that there is hope, and they voice their excitement about our next study. They feel safe. No doubt there will be little they have felt, or done, that I haven't dealt with myself. My strategy is not nuclear science. By being more kingdom-minded we are going to look at things from God's perspective. We are going to see ourselves authentically by focusing on the inside and not the outside.

At least that's my plan.

Nothing that a little faith lift won't help.

four

ROUND AND ROUND WE GO

Kids Who Are Different

Here's to kids who are different,

Kids who don't always get A's,

Kids who have ears

Twice the size of their peers,

And noses that go on for days.

Here's to the kids who are different,

Kids they call crazy or dumb,

Kids who don't fit,

With the guts and the grit,

Who dance to a different drum.

Here's to the kids who are different,

Kids with a mischievous streak,

For when they have grown,

As history has shown,

It's their difference that makes them unique.

AUTHOR: DIGBY WOLFE

Twenty years had passed since my Yankee fan incident, and as a communications teacher, I had created an assignment for my high school juniors. After preparing a list of fun, imaginative questions for kindergarteners, we walked the few blocks to the elementary school and met with the boys and girls for one-on-one interviews. Little did I understand how much would be revealed through those dialogues.

I remember Annie squirming to get comfortable. The concrete bench, a measly 12 inches off the ground, clearly was not designed for seventeen-year-olds but for five-year-olds such as Emily, who wiggled her slight body to the far edge of the shared bench, quiet and noticeably apprehensive, her huge eyes taking everything in.

Annie opened her notebook and nervously clicked her pen, readying for the youngster's answers.

"Emily, what makes snow?" Emily's eyes widened; she knew this answer and couldn't wait to show how smart she was! "That's easy," she blurted, vaulting from the bench. "A fat man sleeps on the clouds. He rolls over and that shakes the snow out."

Annie wrote what she heard, but the kindergartner wasn't finished. Perching on tiptoes, hands raised to the heavens, Emily twinkled her petite fingers back and forth, lower and lower, to help Annie picture the imaginary flakes cascading to the ground.

Emily, now grinning, returned to the bench, this time with less distance between her and her high school interrogator. She turned her knees toward Annie, excited about the questions to come.

As I walked around and observed, what struck me was not the relational bridges being built but the startling contrast between the robust psyches of the kindergarteners and the high schoolers. When my student asked Ryan to sing, I heard the melody from across the courtyard. When little Krista was asked to dance, I had a front row seat to ballet, jazz, and tap. The kindergartners believed that they drew like Picasso, wrote like Shakespeare, and dribbled like Stephen Curry. Their enthusiasm was contagious, their laughter delightful, and there was nothing they couldn't do. Even if they couldn't. They believed otherwise.

Ah, what wonderful times those are, before children begin to believe they aren't good enough.

When I first introduced this assignment, my students weren't particularly excited—probably because it didn't involve a cell phone or Snapchat. Still, my objective was to help (correction: force) these high school juniors to communicate, to converse with different people, regardless of gender, age, or social standing. But afterward, back in the classroom, they couldn't wait to share what they had heard. It was well worth the advanced preparation and became a highlight of my teaching career.

> The kindergartners believed that they drew like Picasso, wrote like Shakespeare, and dribbled like Stephen Curry.

What delighted me was how convincing these five-year-olds were. They *knew* the answer and were overjoyed to share it. Even if they were wrong, they were determined they were right. Sometimes it was all I could do not to laugh aloud as I heard their excited responses. For example:

Q: How old are your parents?
A: Both are 214 years old.

Q: What do you want your wife to look like?
A: My dad.

Q: If you didn't brush your teeth, what would happen?

A: You'd get a hairball.

Q: If you could eat anything, what would it be?
A: My legs, so I wouldn't have to walk.

Q: What does your principal do?
A: Eats and passes out Band-Aids.

Q: What do you worry about?
A: I'm always worried about elephants stomping on me.

Q: How old should you be to marry?
A: 40. And I'm going to marry my mom.

Q: Do you have a pet?
A: I had a fish, but it died so I put it in the trash can.
Q: Did it go to Heaven?
A: No. I told you, it went in the trash can.

Q: How old should you be to drive?
A: 106.

Q: Are you cool?
A: Yes, my daddy calls me cool, and I can pick up heavy things.

Q: Who is Saddam Hussein?
A: Our principal.

Q: What is love?
A: My mom said I'm not supposed to talk about things like that.

You get the picture. These kids had answers, all right, even if they had no clue what they were talking about. They were bold and energized and tickled pink to share their knowledge. And when my students smiled or laughed (except, that is, for the fish story), the youngsters smiled or laughed along. Sadly, all that will change. My students were proof.

Just a few weeks before these interviews, I had asked my class of juniors to raise their hands if they could answer yes to a few questions:

"Can anyone in here draw?"

No one moved. Most avoided eye contact.

"Can anyone sing?"

Same response.

"What about spike a volleyball?"

I might as well have been talking to robots.

"How about weld?"

Actually, robots may have had a little more enthusiasm.

Mind you, I had chosen talents I knew some of my students had. Awards had been given. I saw their gifts; why couldn't they?

Not that I had ever been in that position . . . less than eighty bajillion times.

How about you? When a question is asked in a church class and you know the answer, are you apprehensive to raise your hand? How about group settings when the leader asks for each person to introduce him/herself and your heart starts fluttering? What about how dry your mouth gets when asked to share your testimony? Chances are you're no different than my students. Perhaps your confidence, like theirs, was shaken sometime between the ages of five and seventeen. Perhaps it was at a different age. The point is, the rejection virus spreads whenever someone or something is given the destructive power to take from us that with which God has blessed us. And typically, the perpetrators have their own stories of rejection.

As I reflect on the confidence of those kindergarteners, I can't help but recall that my first, not-so-sentimental fragment of being shunned came somewhere around the age of four after my best friend, Teresa, bragged about her favorite piece of Valentine candy, a small treat that to me looked no different than the fifty others, a perfect row of chalky, Pepto Bismol-flavored, heart-shaped sweets with fuzzy letters haphazardly stamped on their tops.

If I heard it once, I heard it until I wanted to vomit: this was her favorite message, one which she had sought from the first day the V-candies went on sale until that magical day when she opened her twelfth bag and . . . *voila!* There it was.

Sure, there were subtle hints, like a few days earlier when she singled out that silly heart and told me some nonsense about it being the only one she cared about. Or how each time I went to her house she recited over and over and . . . over again how many candy packages she had to open before she found this treasure which, now officially, completed her sacred list.

This was pathetic. Like it was the ark of the covenant or something. Anyway, I ate it.

Teresa wailed like I was sticking pins in her eyes. And her mother came sprinting into her bedroom to see why her sweet baby was acting like . . . well, a baby. With the red dye from the "I Love You" lettering freshly stamped on my tongue, I dared not open my mouth.

"Go on home now," I was told by Teresa's overreacting mother, who coddled her daughter like she had just saved her from the snares of the devil himself. So I promptly did. That was before my friend seriously got back at me.

For several days afterward, Teresa pedaled her tricycle down my sidewalk, but instead of making a 90-degree angle toward my front porch like she did every single day before then, she glared straight ahead like her neck didn't work, playacting like she was clueless I lived there. Until one morning—in a moment of preschooler weakness—she glanced my direction and seemed somewhat pleased that I was standing in our picture window waving like a maniac, dismissing my mother's pleas to stop embarrassing myself. I forgave her—Teresa, not my mother—and we moved on.

Lucky for her.

It was my first memory of being rejected.

Certainly not my last.

The nuns made sure of that. Had they taken a little time to learn about my childhood, they would have been slightly more empathetic. Then again, probably not.

My mom claimed that I bawled nonstop for the first eighteen months of my life. Like most adults, I have no memories of that period, although I sensed that I was born in traumatic times. My brother Jim was a year older than me, and my mom was five months pregnant with my brother David when my dad was diagnosed with multiple sclerosis. I was eight months old when he died, six weeks after he was diagnosed.

My mother's sister, Gladys, and their mother, my grandma, had come by train to Denver from their homes in Missouri to take Jim and me to their houses while my dad was in an iron lung. I stayed with my aunt, and Jim stayed with our grandmother.

Following my father's funeral, Jim and I were reunited with our mom. We lived in Denver during those formative years, but since my mother didn't drive, she relied on her mother-in-law and sister-in-law, who picked her up weekly to go to the grocery store. It was on one such trip that they were hit by a drunk driver and my grandmother was killed. With little physical support, Mom made the decision to relocate to Rich Hill, Missouri, a booming metropolis of about 900, to be near our maternal grandparents. During that time Teresa and I were inseparable . . . well, except for her meltdown period over that stupid piece of candy.

When I was six, we moved again, this time 40 miles away to Fort Scott, Kansas, where Mom found a minimum-wage job as an insurance clerk at the local hospital and enrolled us in Catholic school. For some nutso reason, the nuns at my grade school didn't appreciate me. Actually, I think they wanted to kill me.

It didn't make sense.

I was a delight.

Now let's be clear: this is not nun-bashing. I am in no way qualified to speak about nuns and their lives. Nevertheless . . . I will try.

I think even Mother Teresa would have checked in her habit had she taught the likes of our class. Plus, I'm not sure these Sisters at St. Mary's ever had a vacation. The nunnery was attached to the school, a three-story brick structure with radiator heat (mentioned only because Sister Carlotta occasionally would try to stuff rebels like Kathy and Gerry between its metal cylinders). So . . . that corner at Seventh and Eddy streets became their 24-7 life.

Had I been one of them, and had we cliffs in Kansas, I would have jumped. Fortunately for the nuns, ant hills don't have quite the same effect.

Looking back, I don't get it. I mean, childhood is supposed to be the perfect time of life. Kittens and cupcakes, tap dance classes and Disney movies, candy lipstick and Halloween princess costumes. So many sweet memories.

> Looking back, I don't get it. I mean, childhood is supposed to be the perfect time of life. Kittens and cupcakes, tap dance classes and Disney movies, candy lipstick and Halloween princess costumes.

Returning to school in September was not one of them. The torment started the first day of class when we would stand and tell the class about our summer vacations. My family never went farther than Aunt Gladys's house an hour away in Shell City.

Disneyland? The third-graders had Mickey Mouse ears to prove it. Miami Beach? Wow! Real shells, not just pictures of them, in a shoebox puffy with white sand. The entire project was a remarkably potent tool for young children to feel special. At least, I guess it was.

I assume that show-and-tell assignment was not intended to ignore the few like me whose three-month highlights involved tootling around town on her bike or mooching rides at the rodeo arena from the "really rich" like Diann who had her own horse or hanging out at the public pool mimicking how the older, more popular girls acted. Much of my entertainment came in my own head where I fantasized about being someone people paid attention to. And liked. And, most importantly, considered pretty. Okay, that's a stretch. Let's just say, they didn't want to kill.

Nevertheless, my summer "travels," which included riding a belligerent Shetland pony, competing in watermelon seed-spitting contests, delaying late-night, emergency runs to the spooky outhouse until an explosion was imminent, feeding apples slices to a feeble, thirty-year-old toothless mule, and watching my great aunt train her pet pig—all of which remain some of my favorite childhood memories—brought yawns from the rest of my classmates.

The message seemed clear: *youarepoorandhavenothingtocontributetothisassignmentandnoonecaresaboutyourlife*

I was determined fourth grade would be different.

A powerful lesson in how determination does not equate to outcome.

In that grade there were warning signs I wasn't Sister Delores Marie's favorite. Are you seeing a pattern here? Things like ignoring me when I demurely held up my hand to answer a question, even though she had chosen Chris (a.k.a. "teacher's pet") for the previous ten answers. Or how I never was selected as team captain for our spelling bee even though spelling was one of my favorite subjects and I actually "ex-sailed" at it. (I have clear memories of Sister intentionally mispronouncing a word so I would misspell it, and leering as she banished me to the end of the line. I'm pretty sure her *mwa-ha-ha* snicker gave her great pleasure.)

But I'm over that now. I am.

I really am. Really.

Sort of.

Almost daily when my mother returned home from work, I would recount my abuse and explain how, at any moment, I could come home dead. She, unlike Teresa's overprotective mom, verbalized a worn-out recording: "Now, Patty Honey. I'm sure you're exaggerating. Or you're doing something to intentionally irritate poor Sister Delores Marie."

Can you believe it? Picture the evil stepmother tormenting Cinderella with no one to empathize with her but a mouse.

I needed a mouse, not a mother.

Anyway, back to fourth grade. Our class was responsible for cleaning the candles in the church adjacent to the parochial school. One day Rita, Helen, and I were on duty, working reverently. Seriously! God was hovering and looking for any reason to strike. When we were finished, Rita asked Sister if there was anything else to do. "Yes," she whispered. "Don't hang around with Patty."

Oh. My. Gosh. She! Said! That!

You can't make this stuff up. Well, I guess you can, but I'm not. I might be a Valentine candy thief, but I'm no liar . . . with only a few exceptions . . . like when some bulging lady in Macy's asks me which dress flatters her and none of them do, but because I want her to like me (even though I will never see her again), I choose one and convince her she will look like a supermodel in it, all the while confident her relatives and close friends will talk behind her back. ("What in God's green earth? Just because you can buy it doesn't mean you should wear it!")

At any rate, I'm pretty sure I told my mother about Sister's comment, and I'm pretty sure she thought I made it up. That might not be true, but let's tell ourselves it is. Shortly after that, an angel in the form of my friend Tena's mother came to our house to tell Mom that Tena had told her many stories about how Sister Delores Marie was out to get me. A victory lap around our house was warranted, except we lived directly across the street from the Catholic school/nun's house, and Sister would no doubt see me and say I was behaving like a madwoman—er, girl—and waterboard me the following day in class.

The point is, only then did my mom believe me and set up a visit with Sister Delores Marie to tell her what she had heard. A bold move for my saintly mother who never confronted anyone about any-thing—well, except for me, whom she confronted about *everything*.

But I am over that.

Oh, whatever.

As for further tortures from that school year, I have no recollec-tion. So either (a) Mom was pretty persuasive; or (b) I have a terrible memory.

All I know is, I have chosen to ignore much of that time because . . . well, because I have chosen to ignore much of that time.

five

WILL THE GOOD SAMARITAN PLEASE STAND UP?

You can't blend in when you were born to stand out.
FROM THE MOVIE *WONDER*

Years ago, at a Christian conference I attended, I heard an elderly, frumpish woman speak about how her daily mission was to share Jesus, her best friend and partner, with strangers. She said that on each flight she took she engaged a fellow passenger in his or her occupation, and when the question was reciprocated, she would smile and answer, "I am the daughter of a king." It was a response, she said, that always elicited a conversation. Albeit sometimes an abbreviated one.

She told the audience that periodically she would travel to Las Vegas to speak and would stroll through the casinos. If she heard a frustrated gambler shout out, "Jesus Christ!" she would approach him or her. "Oh, you know him too? Isn't he the best?" She admitted that most of the time her comment was met with grumbles and glares, but it was all about "planting seeds for the Kingdom." She "couldn't help" herself.

Frumpish or not, I wanted her as my BFF. At the end of her talk, we gave her a standing ovation. Her life was about Jesus, not herself, a life demonstrated by her inner beauty—a bold reflection of her relationship with her Lord—which was something we all admired. She shared that her love for her Father and spreading His love was the only thing that mattered regardless of how other people viewed her. She refused to give her consent to the enemy to feel inferior, to hold back from doing God's work.

If we want to do the same, where do we start?

We have to allow ourselves to matter. But matter to whom? We have to figure out whose opinion matters. I mean, it's fun to be appreciated by coworkers or neighbors or our spouse, but their view of us is conditional and has no eternal benefits. The opinion with which we should be most concerned is God's, and to understand that, we have to want to know God so that we know what matters most to Him. This is the first step in understanding our value, and one thing is certain: no one loves us like He does. But how much do we want to want Him?

🏆　🏆　🏆

The legal expert seemed to know the answer before he posed the question. Nevertheless, Jesus, quick to confound those who tried to trap him, was ready. In Luke 10:25-37 we read that the questioner asked Jesus what was necessary to inherit eternal life. When Jesus inquired as to how his interrogator interpreted the Law, he was told, "'Love the Lord your God with all your heart and with all your soul and with all your strength and with all your mind'; and, 'Love your neighbor as yourself.'"

Jesus agreed and added, "Do this and you will live." Not satisfied, the cross examiner asked who his neighbor was. Jesus replied: "A man was going down from Jerusalem to Jericho, when he was attacked by robbers. They stripped him of his clothes, beat him, and went away, leaving him half dead. A priest happened to be going down the same road, and when he saw the man, he passed by on the other side.

"So too, a Levite, when he came to the place and saw him, passed by on the other side. But a Samaritan, as he traveled, came where the man was; and when he saw him, he took pity on him. He went to him and bandaged his wounds, pouring on oil and wine. Then he put the man on his own donkey, brought him to an inn, and took care of him. The next day he took out two denarii and gave them to the innkeeper. 'Look after him,' he said, 'and when I return, I will reimburse you for any extra expense you may have.' Which of these three do you think was a neighbor to the man who fell into the hands of robbers?"

The expert in the law replied, "The one who had mercy on him."

Jesus told him, "Go and do likewise."

Loving the rejected had a special place in Jesus' ministry.

A few years before I retired from teaching and directing plays in high school, I was asked to modernize and direct "The Good Samaritan" skit for our local Red Cross prayer breakfast. Wanting to make a real impact, I solicited the help of our new debate coach, Brian Weilert, to act the part of a beggar outside of the college cafeteria venue where the meeting would be held. Brian was new to our community, so there was little chance anyone would recognize him.

His role was to sit under a tree and ask for money. From a cafeteria window, my acting students and I watched the reactions from civic and church leaders as they arrived and neared where Brian begged. Most seemed aghast that someone so filthy would dare interrupt their casual conversations, and others actually shoulder-checked their sidewalk mates in order to get away.

At one point, one of my actors overheard a cafeteria worker asking her boss to call the police because the guests were complaining about a bum outside. Fortunately, I was able to intervene before that call was made.

Once inside, all the guests seemed to forget the outside intrusion as they took their seats at beautifully decorated tables and visited with one another during their breakfast buffet. When it was our turn to perform, Dillon, a small-framed freshman, walked onstage and began to count his lunch money. Along came two thugs—students who took my class only to learn stage combat—who bullied Dillon, took his change, and beat him up, leaving him lying on the ground.

Then entered two preppy cheerleaders on their way to practice. When they noticed the wounded, "bleeding" boy, they began gagging and ran away yelling, "Gross." And "disgusting." And "now my day is ruined" and "we're probably going to get a disease."

Following the cheerleaders came a Bible-carrying student dressed in a suit and walking speedily to his destination. When he neared Dillon, he bent down to see if the injured teen was breathing but quickly apologized, announcing that if he helped, he would be late for the Fellowship of Christian Athletes' meeting. As president of the organization, he said, he had to make a good impression.

Last, a football player entered, vowing that he sincerely wanted to help, and had it not been for the recent muscle strain in his back, he would have offered assistance.

That was Brian's cue to enter the room, his crooked limb braced under his arm as a crutch, his "Please Help" sign draped around his neck. From my vantage point I could see the horrorstruck expressions of the prayer breakfast guests. They all seemed to be wondering which of their tablemates would be bold enough to direct the beggar outside. It was a cricket's moment as Brian took his time weaving through the crowd and ultimately ended up onstage, kneeling beside the wounded young man.

Brian then helped Dillon up, reached in his pocket, and took the few coins he had (none from the attendees, I might add) and gave them to the "wounded" teen. They embraced. That was my cue to walk onstage.

The sense of relief demonstrated from the audience when I introduced them to the "Good Samaritan," our high school's new debate coach, was dramatic. At that moment the nine cast members, including Brian, took their places across the stage, each delivering a memorized segment of this ageless poem:[5]

1. God won't ask what kind of car you drove. He'll ask how many people you drove who didn't have transportation.

2. God won't ask the square footage of your house. He'll ask how many people you welcomed into your home.

3. God won't ask about the clothes you had in your closet. He'll ask how many you helped clothe.

4. God won't ask what your highest salary was. He'll ask if you compromised your character to obtain it.

5. God won't ask what your job title was. He'll ask if you performed your job to the best of our ability.

6. God won't ask how many friends you had. He'll ask how many people to whom you were a friend.

7. God won't ask in what neighborhood you lived. He'll ask how you treated your neighbors.

8. God won't ask about the color of your skin. He'll ask about the content of your character.

What I love about this poem is that the writer seemed to get that God won't ask any questions about possessions or status or looks. He cares about our character. And that's what we should care about too. But how much do we want to care about what God cares about? The best part of this story came a week later when the head of the Red Cross called me and said that, following the prayer breakfast, their organization received more donations than ever before.

Returning to Luke, one has to question at what point "love thy neighbor as thyself" becomes a lifestyle. I would suggest only after we love God above all else. Hundreds of books have been written on the subject, but rarely do we see that kind of love in action. Actually, rarely do we desperately want God to be anything but a footnote in our lives, even though—and yes, I repeat myself—no one loves us like He does.

Her name was, let's say, Sarah. Sarah was quirky. I met her when I was substitute teaching in a Texas middle school math class. As I passed out the students' worksheets, the paraprofessional aide assigned to the class whispered that Sarah would need two papers, one for her and one for her imaginary friend, Adrianne, who sat behind her in the empty desk.

The aide continued with more instructions: I was not to correct Sarah for turning around to "translate" to Adrianne whatever I was teaching.

Okaayy??

I had no idea imaginary friends could survive past preschool. Except for my friend Linda's pal, who sometime in elementary school had gotten into a taxi and driven off a cliff, all my other friends' make-believe sidekicks had disappeared by the time they were five. But for this thirteen-year-old, Adrianne was the real deal.

I observed Sarah inquisitively. She would work a few problems and then, with no regard for what her classmates thought, turn to help her "friend" catch up. When the bell rang and Sarah packed her supplies, she giddily shared with Adrianne what was going to happen the rest of the day. It was obvious she delighted in her best buddy.

A month later while subbing in the same school, I was in the teachers' lounge when that same math para entered. I inquired about Sarah.

"You wouldn't believe what happened," I was told.

It seems that some ornery boys in the class decided to play a trick on Sarah and created their own imaginary friends who bullied Adrianne and "caused a fight" with her. After that incident, the teacher announced that no more imaginary friends were allowed in the classroom. They would have to wait in the hall until class was dismissed. Sarah was devastated. For days she sulked and refused to do her work. The school psychologist was called as school officials sought a solution.

But then a strange thing happened.

When Sarah came to school the next day, the para watched her carefully place her backpack beside her desk, slowly open its zipper, and secretively help "someone" out.

Sarah had sneaked Adrianne into the classroom.

Once again, Sarah was attentive, smiling, and full of energy. She was her old self.

I occasionally think of Sarah, not only because her story was so bizarre, but because I want to be equally as desperate to take Jesus with me wherever I go. Because without Him I will feel a great void. Because I absolutely delight in Him. Because people recognize a visible difference when He's with me. Because I don't care what other people think of me when I make it obvious we are inseparable.

And Jesus, unlike Adrianne, isn't imaginary.

He is the real, real deal.

When I speak to Christian women I sometimes challenge them with this introduction: "Write on your paper three things that absolutely delight you, things you look forward to, things that make you smile. For me, it's watching the deer nestle in my front yard, it's teaching my grandchildren how to swing dance, and it's riding a horse that doesn't run me into a fence."

After giving them a few minutes, I encourage them to share their responses with their neighbor. Then I ask them, "How many of you had God or Jesus on your list?" Typically, if there are three hundred women present, five will raise their hands. Granted, I did not prompt them into a spiritual answer with the personal examples I gave. I want their responses to be real. I want God to be real and as necessary as Adrianne is to Sarah.

Let's face it. Our world is not what it was three years ago when no one knew what impact Covid-19 would have on all of us, when our churches would be forced to shut their doors, Bible studies would find Zoom as the only substitute for human connection, and we would have front row seats to what loneliness could cause. My counselor friends were swamped, hearing the same story from every patient who felt hopeless as finger-pointing over Covid and vaccines caused friendships to dissolve and raging arguments to ensue. Sermons online turned to "Is This the End Times?" and "Where Is God in This Mess?"

If ever there was a time to lean in to God, this was it, yet I'm not sure many used the pandemic to develop an intimate relationship with the One they need to love above all else. Covid has given us the perfect time to get to know Him as He deserves to be known, and it is impossible to love Him if we don't. But we must want to *want* to love Him.

If we are to get to the place where God will be the only One who defines us, we *must* know who He is and acknowledge that He has made a life-changing impact on our soul. He cannot merely be our insurance policy when times get tough. He deserves a love far beyond what we feel for our family members or best friends. A bride and bridegroom kind of love so that we wouldn't want to spend one second without Him partnering in our thoughts, words, and actions. In C.S. Lewis's book *A Grief Observed*, Lewis wrote something I need to recite several times a day: "I need Christ, not something that resembles him."[6]

We must start by being honest about how much we actually love God. "Radically honest," as my friend, author Virelle Kidder, describes in her writing. "Facing ourselves honestly, sins and stupidity included, is huge. It's also the launchpad for renewal."[7]

If you're with me on this, you're welcome.

God adores us. I don't know why. What I do know is that we don't deserve anything from Him. If we're honest, we'll acknowledge that we must use this opportunity as a starting point for renewal. And here's the beauty of it: all we have to do is ask.

In the book of Exodus we learn that God called for a one-on-one visit with Moses where He assigned him the responsibility of bringing the Israelites out of Egypt and leading them to the Promised Land. God listened as Moses desperately produced five excuses as to why he was not qualified.

- I'm inadequate; I'm not a leader.
"Who am I that I should go to Pharaoh, and that I should bring the children of Israel out of Egypt?" (Exodus 3:11)

- I'm inadequate; I don't know enough.
Then Moses said to God, "Indeed, when I come to the children of Israel and say to them, 'The God of your fathers has sent me to you,' and they say to me, 'What is His name?' what shall I say to them?" (Exodus 3:13)

- I'm inadequate; I won't appear trustworthy.
Then Moses answered and said, "But suppose they will not believe me or listen to my voice; suppose they say, 'The Lord has not appeared to you'" (Exodus 4:11).

- I'm inadequate; I have no charisma.
Then Moses said to the Lord, "O my Lord, I am not eloquent, neither before nor since You have spoken to Your servant; but I am slow of speech and slow of tongue" (Exodus 4:10).

- I'm inadequate, plain and simple.
But he said, "O my Lord, please send by the hand of whomever else You may send" (Exodus 4:13).

Can't you just hear the whining escalate? But aren't we all guilty? This is serious stuff. Excusing our sense of inadequacy annuls the truth that God offered His Son so we might have life and have it to the full (yes, a *full* life, a *renewed* life), yet when we fail to live up to God's expectations, we pooh-pooh the ultimate sacrifice and value Satan's perspective instead. We settle for a half-life or a quarter-life, maybe even an eighth-life, but certainly not a full life. And then we wonder why we have no joy.

Lord, help us. Please.

It's time to get real with God. Don't dismiss the transparency required to begin your journey into Kingdom living. Admit how you have hung onto feelings of being overlooked. Unworthy. Forgotten. Dismissed. Neglected. Unvalued. Acknowledge how you have rejected God's words that call you into a life of abundance. How you have settled, tragically, for so much less.

Romans 8:6-8 (*The Message*) gives us a warning: *Obsession with self in these matters is a dead end; attention to God leads us out into the open, into a spacious, free life. Focusing on the self is the opposite of focusing on God. Anyone completely absorbed in self ignores God, ends up thinking more about self than God. That person ignores who God is and what he is doing. And God isn't pleased at being ignored.*

Realness is required. For some reason I have yet to understand, Christians deserve Oscars when it comes to faking it—especially spiritually. We raise our hands in worship, text "PTL" when we read of God's blessings, and maybe even slap an Ichthus sticker on the back of our cars. We are constantly on our toes "performing" like Christians. Heaven forbid we ever admit that we're in a faith slump or our life isn't all hunky-dory. I don't get it. Jesus is a resurrected Messiah, no matter how much I fail to represent him well. Yes, we sin. We fight ugly thoughts. We have doubts. We struggle with holiness.

And if you don't, please let me know your secret.

58

Even Mother Teresa had times of depression and wrote her superiors, begging for help. This 1953 excerpt is from what is referred to as the "Dark Letters": "Such deep longing for God — and . . . repulsed — empty — no faith — no love — no zeal. (Saving) souls holds no attraction — Heaven means nothing — pray for me please that I keep smiling at Him in spite of everything."[8] (As an aside, I applaud the Vatican for not disposing of Mother Teresa's letters, even though she asked that they do so.)

Sometimes, sweet people, there is a huge disconnect between being a Christian and being Christlike. Sometimes, sweet people, if we're honest, we will admit we aren't perfect. We get edgy. Sometimes we get downright disagreeable. We get frustrated. It's true. So here's some honesty: Sometimes my husband Dave makes me cranky. Actually, more than sometimes. I'd like to blame it on Covid, but I can't. Like when I'm doing a crossword puzzle and have a sports question that I know he knows, and it's the last answer I need, and he thinks it's funny to be uncooperative.

"Dave, what's a four-letter word for the last name of the man who invented football?" Predictably, hubby will say "rhinoceros" and about five other ten-letter answers, just to get under my skin. But the other day he outdid himself. The alarm clock had just gone off and, still half-asleep, we met in the bathroom and gave each other a quick "we-haven't-brushed-our-teeth-yet" kiss. He then asked me this question: "Did our stomachs just meet before our lips did?" He. Seriously. Said. That.

You can understand why—even though I love him silly—I periodically feel a strong need to smack him silly, can't you?

The sad, truthful thing is, I know Christian women who have been asked by young wives struggling with their spouses if they ever have troublesome times in their marriage, and they say, "Praise, God, no! My husband is my soulmate and best friend and God put us together to be a team." How precious is that? I mean, if ever there's a "goody, goody, gumdrop" response, that would be it.

Along with wanting to stick a darning needle in my eye, if you give me that kind of answer, I will vow to never again come to you for marital advice because you just reinforced that I am an ungodly loser-wife who needs to lose some belly fat.

Nobody has a perfect marriage. Nobody has a perfect faith. Sometimes we're on the mountaintop, and sometimes we're in the valley. And we all know which has more growth. Admit it. And grow.

Being transparent is necessary if we are to become honest with God, for then we reveal our inadequacies and ask Him to fill us with *His* thoughts about us. We throw off the shroud of secrecy that has kept us masquerading as something we are not and work on . . . realness. Trust me: when we no longer feign a confidence that we know is fake—when we no longer are concerned about becoming a target for someone's rejection—we are liberated. Being open about who we are protects and enhances relationships by allowing others to do the same.

In the high school theater class I taught, my beginner actors were taught how to "look the part," how to use their bodies and gestures and facial expressions to bring a role alive. My advanced actors took it to a much higher level. They would "become" the character. They understood: how would they feel/react/respond if they were inside the skin of the individual they portrayed?

The first group would wear the WWJD bracelets. (Well, actually, probably not because those wrist wraps are totally outdated, but you get the point.) These teens would be the starving actors who are exhausted physically, emotionally, and spiritually from the roles they play trying to impress coworkers, friends, pew-mates, and even God.

The second group wouldn't have to ask what Jesus would do; it would be intrinsic to their nature. Just as a cat doesn't stop to question if it should chase a ball of twine, so the Christian should not have to ask how she/he is supposed to act; it would just happen because that's who she or he is. Jesus should emanate from every pore.

Here's a nugget of reality: In both acting and real life, faking it is much easier than being it. Sooooo not our fault; thank you, Adam and Eve. Like almost everything else, they seriously are to blame. Remember them hiding after they blew it and ate from the Tree of Knowledge of Good and Evil? Before that they walked around naked and shameless, but from that nibble on, they lost confidence in who they were created to be. They chose their own design over that of their Designer.

Sin entered the landscape, but guess what! Jesus overcame sin. He defeated it on the cross, and we now have the freedom to be un-ashamed and honest. Not in the Genesis, strut-around-naked sort of way (which seriously makes me break out in hives, just thinking about it), but figuratively speaking.

So why don't we believe it?

Acknowledging our failings doesn't mean we stay there. Quite the contrary. If I falter, if I'm weak and tempted, if I'm feeling inadequate, God will be there to pick me up and tend to my broken heart. But geez Louise, we need to stop hiding from Him and tell Him how we feel. It's not like He doesn't know anyway. He's omnipotent. Nothing escapes His loving eyes. He wants an open relationship, not a make-believe one.

So here's your homework: Get honest. Be transparent. Get real. Talk to God. If this is troublesome for you and you can't put your feelings into words, ask God to show you areas in which you are not allowing Him to be your confidence (or, as my friend Diane calls it, your Godfidence). Ask Him to help you want to want Him. You will make His day!

Write down where you feel inadequate. Is it as a mother? A wife? A church member? An employee? A volunteer? Is it your looks or your intelligence or your social standing? Is it because you've allowed others to place expectations on you that you can't meet? Whatever the reason, share your inadequacies with your Heavenly Father. He gets it. He wants you to celebrate His design on how He created you. And trust me on this: nobody knows you like He does.

In case you're banging your head into a wall right now, totally confused about what you need to say, here's a prayer that might jump-start your desire to get real.

Glorious Father, I have spent far too many years trying to be something I'm not. I've bought into Satan's lies and find myself knowing there is more. Please help me love You above all else. Help me to strive to know You the way You deserve to be known. Help me to be ever thankful for You giving me Your son to die in my place so that I will give You Your rightful place. You, Heavenly Father, are the only audience that counts. Help me live accordingly. Help me want to want you.

six

A LESSON FROM THE ACADEMY AWARDS

You may not control all the events that happen to you,
but you can decide not to be reduced by them.
MAYA ANGELOU

Following our taco time, I hand my Bible study girls a stack of the latest fashion magazines. I tell them that they are to leaf through the pages and list the physical qualities represented.

"Thin." "Gorgeous hair." "Beautiful eyes." "Great clothes." "Jewelry to die for." "Perfect."

"And who of you," I ask them, "sees yourself just as perfect as you see these movie stars?" I might as well ask them to shoot heroin.

I continue. "What if your personal assistant followed you around, held a dome light over your head and blew your hair with a wind machine? Oh, yeah, let's not forget the professional makeup artists and airbrush technicians and masseuses. And the surgeons ready on command to suck, stick, plant, and break whatever it is that needs perfected, and the personal trainers to make sure you continue looking sucked, stuck, planted, and broken. After all, no one ever said beauty is pain-free. Couldn't you then be just as beautiful?"

I'm on a roll. "Is there any chance we are confusing cover models with role models? Actually, I'm not so sure most of those celebrities aren't pretty miserable. I can name on one hand the number of gorgeous, famous movie stars whose marriages have survived into their golden years."

Of course, I can't name them (though I know my assertion is basically true), so I switch topics.

I tell a story that actress Jamie Lee Curtis shared during a television interview. She and her husband were at the Academy Awards and Jamie, who had recently undergone liposuction and some facial surgery, asked her spouse to look around the room and pick out the most beautiful woman there. It took him no time to choose Jessica Tandy, a gray-haired, ninety-plus-year-old woman who was up for an Oscar. Shocked, Jamie asked her husband why. "Because she's the only one here who is real," he said, according to Curtis. Jamie said that was the last time she would ever go under the knife.

And yes, this story gave me much personal satisfaction.

As the girls continue to leaf through the magazines, I ask them, "Would you change anything about your appearance if you could?" As quickly as you can say "Botox," they ramp up, listing a dozen things they want corrected, all dealing with their appearance, and all of which I find ridiculous: Too fat. High forehead. Crooked nose. Too fat. Thin hair. Too short. Ugly feet. Too fat. Skinny lips. Too fat.

Oh, you sweet little dears, I want to say. A day is coming when your chins will outnumber your wrinkles, your muffin tops will mock your Spandex, you'll flat-iron the creases in your eyelids to apply shadow, orthotics will replace spike heels, and your bones will sound like Rice Krispies even when in your Barcalounger. And that's just the beginning!

But I don't.

Instead, I say this: "First, look at each other. Do you see a high forehead, a crooked nose, a fat body, skinny lips, or thin hair on anyone in this group? Are you surprised these girls sitting beside you have these body image insecurities?" They're all shocked because they know each other well and see each other as so "together."

This is crippling. These girls weren't *always* broken. Just a few years before, this group of self-proclaimed rejects had been innocent kindergarten princesses who twirled confidently in their new dresses, giggling and pirouetting when they looked in the mirror. Girls who God intended to be confident in the gifts He had given them had permitted people or circumstances to squash their self-worth. And they were doing nothing to push back against the weight of failure.

A.W. Tozer's metaphor says it well in his inspirational book *The Pursuit of God*: "It is a solemn thing, and no small scandal in the Kingdom, to see God's children starving while actually seated at the Father's table."[9] Our Father was offering these teens a life of confidence and joy, yet they thumbed their petite little noses—the ones they saw as flaring and unsymmetrical and way too large—at His treasured gifts.

> Our Father was offering these teens a life of confidence and joy, yet they thumbed their petite little noses—the ones they saw as flaring and unsymmetrical and way too large—at His treasured gifts.

Perhaps you can relate. You realize, like I once did, that although you would never utter the words, your feelings and actions call God a liar. You don't *honestly* believe He is trustworthy no matter how He leans into your life to prove otherwise. You're told that no one will ever love you like He does, that He loves you immeasurably more than you love Him, but you're not convinced. He'll test you; you can bank on it. Cancer, bankruptcy, divorce . . . and there's always that dreaded "called-to-Africa" thing.

None of our stories are identical. No doubt we all have our own "show-and-tell" memories. Satan makes sure of it. In spite of his tactics, I am excited about what lies ahead. This evening these teens seem more transparent, the first step to changing some destructive habits they've been developing. Little do they know how much we have in common, for the road to my life's journey also had been potholed with struggles of insecurity. The difference was, as I aged, I decided to be honest—there's that word again—about my inadequacies and refused to let them define me. I was willing to share my shortcomings with others, and I had learned not to take life so seriously.

Most importantly, I had come to care more about what God thinks of me and less about the opinions of others.

It just took me a long time to get there. Two obnoxious eighth-graders and a snooty neighbor didn't help.

🏆 🏆 🏆

To add a few more ingredients to the grade school "humiliation pie" I was learning to eat, there were always the upper classmen put on this earth to squash what little self-worth we eleven-year-olds actually had. One of my most vivid memories involved two of them, a missed recess, and a pair of shoes.

When my two brothers and I were young, we always knew school was getting close because our mother would take us downtown to buy new shoes, a dress pair and a school pair. Not hand-me-downs; the real thing. My fifth-grade year I talked Mom into letting me get a pair of black patent-leather shoes with French heels. I tried them on with dainty white anklets and felt seriously stunning as I blundered gracelessly up and down the rows of boxed foot apparel, thrilled with the tapping sound my new "church shoes" made on the polished linoleum. The rest of the day was occupied with happy, anticipatory hours (one can dream!) as I practiced acting ladylike and refined.

The next day was Sunday; I flitted onto the Miss America runway; some people, with less imagination, might have known it as a church aisle. I would have waved to my fans had my mother not been watching me with eyebrow arched, a look for which I was the recipient far too often. Actually, in my case, I think her arched brow was penciled on daily in that configuration as a "Don't you dare, Patty Ann" reminder.

The following morning, I pleaded with my mother to let me wear my new best friends to school. She refused. And I refused . . . to give up. After resorting to wailing, I convinced my poor mother, who had been unfortunate enough to birth an insufferable daughter, to give in "but just this once."

Oh, happy day! First the anklets, rolled perfectly so the lace lay flat and not curled, then the Cinderella slippers, and finally the test: the mirror. I was pretty. I soon would have all my classmates crowding around me, wanting me to be their partner in jump rope or, better yet, asking if *they* could push *me* on the merry-go-round instead of insisting that I do the pushing since I was a head taller than the boys.

Mickey Mouse ears: take that!

That morning I arrived at school more than punctually, not unlike the timing with which our family arrived at mass every single, solitary Sunday. (My mother believed it was necessary to show up thirty minutes before the other churchgoers so we could sit alone in our pew and stare at each other in our dress clothes.) Anyway, sometime in the first hour or two of school, according to my slightly unreliable memory, the predictable happened. The nun *happened* to look my way when I *happened* to be talking and I was told I had to stay in at recess. That day I didn't care, because even staying in at recess can be fun if you're pretty.

There I sat, all alone, legs crossed, rhythmically swinging my foot up just above the front of my desk, affording me the perfect view of my reflection in my patent-leather shoes. Through the corner of my eye I noticed a couple of eighth-grade girls walking by the classroom door. I flipped my feet a little higher, just in case they had missed their chance to envy what I had and they didn't, but instead of "oohs" and "aahs" from the hallway, I heard giggling. I stared as the eighth-grade troublemakers backed into the open doorway, pointed at my feet, and began laughing hysterically. I had no idea what was so funny. Perhaps it was the anklets. Perhaps it was just a gangly, awkward, eleven-year-old klutz with size eight shoes trying to fit in. Perhaps it was just who they were. (The last part I didn't believe until years later.)

The point is, I am in my seventies and still remember that incident as if it happened this morning. I remember the heartless look on the two girls' faces, and I remember not feeling pretty again for a very, very long time. It was a life lesson, but it didn't end there, for even now there are those moments of insecurity. My patent-leather shoe experience just masquerades in different forms.

The only difference between then and now is that I now recognize the whisperer . . . and it isn't my Creator. It just took me a long time to figure that out.

Even when I speak, I have to reject a faint whisper reminding me that I am incompetent. I'm not smart enough. I'm not young enough. I'm not funny enough. And I'm definitely not holy enough. No person exists who is less qualified than I. Even now, when I walk into a room full of strangers, I'm a little uncomfortable. Even now, when I look in a mirror, I wonder who replaced me with an aging imposter.

The only difference between then and now is that I now recognize the whisperer . . . and it isn't my Creator. It just took me a long time to figure that out.

My neighbor didn't help.

Across the alley from our rental house where I grew up lived a wealthy couple that owned an exclusive men's clothing store. Their home, a three-story, imposing brick structure with a meticulously landscaped yard and majestic leaded windows, was truly one of the grandest buildings in our town. Having never been inside such a house, I could only dream of what it would be like to live in that kind of luxury. I was one who bragged to my friends when my mother saved enough money to turn our utility room into my bedroom where, as long as the door was open, I had heat.

Our neighbor's only child, Patty, was a year older than me, and nightly she, some other neighbor kids, my brothers, and I would play Kick the Can on our sidewalk until the street lights came on. If we needed a drink, we would go inside my house for one. Patty's house was off limits, although I was too dimwitted to figure that out, in spite of a few hints.

One day, for example, I knocked at her back door to see if Patty could come out and play. Her mother greeted me and explained that she was upstairs; I could wait if I would like. This was my chance! I finally would see how the super-rich lived. As I started to step inside, an arm blocked my entrance. "You can stay outside. Patty will be right out," her mother said rather testily.

I suppressed that memory until I was 45 years old and our family had moved back to Fort Scott from Texas so my brother David could coach our teenage sons in baseball. With few homes on the market, we rented for several months, but then Patty's former house went up for sale. There had been a few other owners since we had been neighbors, but because it was in our price range, my husband and I made arrangements to check it out.

Walking in the front door, Dave and I both were awed by its grandeur. The spacious living room boasted perfectly stained, hardwood floors with a stately brick fireplace at its far end. The dining room was equally as breathtaking with its built-in mahogany cabinetry supporting leaded glass doors.

Leaving that room, we entered the kitchen through a solid wood, swinging door. Immediately I was at the back door in that 1959 exchange, reliving those moments with Patty's mother. Turning to Dave, all I could say was "Wow."

That's it.

Just "Wow."

He thought I was complimenting the room. Not even close. I remained silent while Dave opened and shut the cabinets and checked the faucet's water pressure.

We finished inspecting the rooms on the second and third floors and then took a quick peek at the basement. As we were leaving, the current owner made small talk by filling us in on what happened to Patty's family. It was tragic. Years before, her father had passed away, the business began failing, her mother was forced to move into an apartment, where she died penniless, and Patty pretty much disappeared. No doubt the years spent in that upscale, elegant house had not been anything close to the loving memories my family shared in our unpretentious, sixty-five-dollars-a-month, clapboard-sided rental across the alley.

Dave and I bought that house, and when I told him the story of not being in the same social class as my neighbor, he and I became more determined than ever that this house would be used as a welcoming place for anyone who came to visit. And when they came, they would know they were valued.

Not surprisingly, God gave us many opportunities to make sure that happened.

seven

OUT ON A LIMB...
AND NOT IN A FUN WAY

You are you. Now, isn't that pleasant?
Dr. Seuss

Psalm 139:13 calls for careful reading: *For you created my inmost being; you knit me together in my mother's womb.*

For far too many years, I questioned if God got His knit and purl confused with His cable and switch.

Tall, skinny, and freckled would have described me perfectly during my elementary and junior high years. Visualize five feet of legs with a head attached. Years later, when I brought Dave home to introduce him to my family, my brothers thought it hysterical to bring out my seventh-grade picture and share it, further humiliating me by telling my fiancé that they breathed a sigh of relief when someone in high school finally was desperate enough to ask me for a date. (We were close like that.) The truth is, for the first fifteen years of my life, I wasn't too sure about my future, either.

Growing up poor and fatherless has a way of validating one's lack of worth. Since our view of God is based on our view of our earthly fathers, I struggled from early on with a distorted view of what God was like.

My saintly mother did the best she could, and with the help of my grandparents (who brought sacks full of groceries each Sunday) and my Denver cousins who sent me their hand-me-down clothes, we managed to survive on Mom's minimum-wage salary. Of course, having no television or car for the first few years we were in Kansas set us apart. People on welfare had those luxuries, and I remember questioning how my classmates' parents stayed home and had so much more than we did. I found myself envious of them, fancying how many better things we could have if my mom quit work.

> Growing up poor and fatherless has a way of validating one's lack of worth.

She would have none of it, teaching my brothers and me lessons like "hard work pays off."

"Well, not enough to buy a car or television," I dramatically reminded her.

My mother refused to date, committing herself to our deceased father and us. Because of that, she stayed home every evening and weekend so we couldn't get away with anything fun.

She followed through when she threatened to wash our mouths out with soap.

She knew who our friends were and what we were doing with them.

She insisted that if we said we would be gone for an hour, we were gone for an hour . . . or less.

Mom took great pride in our rented home, and when she saved enough money, she carpeted and wallpapered it. She broke the child labor laws and made us do chores. We had to wash and dry dishes, iron, put jeans on stretchers, make our beds, cook, vacuum the floor, clean the knickknacks, empty the trash, and mow the lawn with a push mower. Saturday mornings were dedicated to scouring our house, and we couldn't go outside and play until our duties were checked. I think she would lie awake at night thinking of ways to convince us to run away.

My mother was a party pooper. She never joined me in complaining about our senile neighbor but, instead, took her to church with us and let her sit in the same pew where she would make weird gas noises that had an embarrassingly adverse effect on the kind of attention I sought. Especially if cute Glenn, my St. Mary's school crush, was sitting with his family anywhere close. My mom refused to gossip, no matter how true it was, and said totally uncool things like, "Unless you have walked in their shoes . . . " which I sort of wanted to do, considering theirs probably were much more stylish than mine.

I didn't get it then, but there were countless times when there would be three pieces of cake left and she would tell Jim, David, and me she wasn't in the mood for cake. That, of course, made my brothers and me thrilled because then it was every boy/girl for him/herself. Style wasn't important to my mom, yet she had no problem spending her savings on material to make me a new blouse whenever I, true to my long-suffering flair, whined because I had "nothing to wear."

My mother lived to be 95 and somehow managed to survive without a credit card. Everything was paid for in cash, or it wasn't bought. I thought that was how all adults lived until the day I discovered there was a better way.

At the age of thirteen I walked to town one Saturday afternoon and lucked upon "the perfect outfit." Thanks to my baby-sitting jobs I had saved a little money, but there was a slight problem: I didn't have *enough* money. Fortunately, the salesclerk had the answer. "Credit." I could "take the clothes home and pay later." Wow! *I must have been awfully good to deserve this gargantuan miracle*, I thought, because it was no secret that cool clothes could cover a multitude of insecurities.

When I leisurely walked in the front door with my shopping bag, Mom asked what I had bought. I eagerly explained the "buy-now-pay-later" concept and shared with her how my life would never be the same. She agreed and immediately set about negating my giddiness, and she didn't do it with any "let's discuss this" rhetoric. After instructing me to get into the car—yes, we finally had a car!—she drove me back to the clothing store where she informed the sales clerk that I was never, ever allowed to purchase anything from that store again unless I had the cash to cover it.

And speaking of "never, ever," I would never, ever be seen in public again.

My mean mother had scarred me for life. It was just one more validation that my elementary years spent searching for a morsel of dignity were the norm and not the exception.

🏆　🏆　🏆

As a child I did all I could to persuade God not to kill me. I desperately worked to convince Him I was worthy of His love, that I wasn't really as naughty as I acted most of my waking hours. I even added up my sins (after being told that each time I whispered when the nun's back was turned, I was violating a commandment). With actual numbers. "Four-thousand, one hundred and thirty-seven times I disobeyed this month," I confessed to the priest.

He didn't seem surprised.

For bonus points I took my guardian angel to the playground and swung her. I tried not to flirt with boys except, of course, for Glenn who . . . *helloooooo*, was soooooo cute, knew how to dangle from tree limbs, and even had a tooth knocked out in a fistfight. He was such a "boy's boy" that surely God couldn't expect me not to just *look* at him.

I feared eternity and was convinced that with my luck—not to mention my propensity to disobey—I would pass away with a mortal sin on my soul and burn in the *bowels* of hell forever. Now, hell was one thing, but the bowels of hell? Gross! What were the odds that a troublemaker like me could die during one of my truly few holy moments, like when I was in church praying—and actually meaning it—and not sneaking pathetically needy glances at Glenn?

Answer: Not good.

Because of that, I spent far too many years trying to earn spiritual merit badges to impress God. (I know, bad theology.)

It wasn't until I was almost 30 that I was told I was loved unconditionally. God wasn't out to get me. There were no degrees of sin. Rolling my eyes wasn't a "1," and plotting to murder my brother who had smashed margarine in my hair wasn't a "10."

God was all about forgiveness, and no matter how much I labored to earn my way into Heaven, I was wasting my time. It was all about what Jesus had done two thousand years ago. Learning that I could do nothing to save myself, that it wasn't about my works but about God's grace, unearnable by definition, was revolutionary to me, not to mention an experience that secured a default place in my heart for the rest of my life: God loves me.

I had a chance after all.

Too bad I didn't get that message several years earlier. Maybe then a little Easter blunder wouldn't have been quite so traumatizing. Let me explain.

In elementary school, my St. Mary's classmates and I prepared ahead of time to answer the notorious pre-Lenten question, "What are you giving up for Lent?" My friends' answers— "candy," "my bicycle," "ice cream," *Bonanza* (the old hit western TV show)—paled in comparison to mine. Naturally, no one was dimwitted enough to say "nothing"—especially when the nuns had us stand at attention beside our desks and share our answers. It was a spiritual opportunity to one-up each other.

Probably because of jealousy, my noble sacrifice never received the acclamations it deserved, even though mine seriously eclipsed everyone else's. I would give up the one thing I craved, the one snack upon which I was dependent for happiness: salt on ice cubes. Had my classmates not eaten for forty days, their sacrifice wouldn't come close to mine. They, unlike me, had no idea what withdrawals were all about.

For the entire Lenten season, it was all I could do not to sneak an ice cube since the entire procedure took such little effort. Five simple steps to paradise: (1) remove the ice tray from the freezer; (2) pull the silver lever to loosen the cubes; (3) place the ice into one of those colored aluminum cups; (4) add salt granules; (5) lick away.

I get goosebumps just thinking about it.

The first year I proudly broadcast my answer in class, not-a-little-agitated Sister looked at me like I was a whack-a-doodle, told me this wasn't a joke, and had me sit down. (Are you understanding my embarrassment here? I mean, who's going to double-cross God by fibbing when grace points are involved? Not to mention violate a sacred Lenten oath knowing that would be justification for one of those infamous "bowels of hell" lectures.)

At any rate, how was it possible to screw up Lent? Was I the only one of God's creation who could be hopeless at fasting? Was this yet one more sin which deserved a visit to the confessional? Jesus, have mercy on my soul! Since I feared hell for a number of other sins I recurrently committed, adding this biggie just might do me in.

The nuns had no idea what discipline it took to imitate holiness. At least I should have been given credit for that. Nope. By the time I entered seventh grade, it became apparent just how unholy they thought I was.

To the best of my somewhat-exaggerated recollection, Sister Carlotta was eight feet tall and 150 years old when we had her as our seventh- and eighth-grade teacher. Both classes shared a room, so while Sister was teaching one grade, the other would/should be doing schoolwork.

Now that I'm older, I have tremendous empathy for the poor woman just trying to serve the Lord while a group of hellions ran amok in her classroom. There were, however, a few habits (pun intended) of hers that could have used some alterations. Like how she kept a roll of toilet paper on her desk and frequently divvied out one square per student for us to blow our noses simultaneously.

Seriously! We were 13- and 14-year-olds—halfway to being mediocrely mature—and no one had the guts to revolt, to refuse to be part of the tissue-blowing chorus, to stand up and announce we deserved more—like at least two squares—or, better yet, that our sinuses were void of any gross mucus to blow. We were lemmings off a cliff, following along . . . timidly. (I'd say "spineless" except lemmings are vertebrates, so my metaphor kind of falls apart here, but you get the point.)

A better word to describe us during those days is petrified.

For good reason.

Each school morning we attended mass, and for certain funerals we sang from the choir loft while Sister Carlotta played the monstrous pipe organ. Even though seated on her bench behind us, her lofty leers of contempt managed to pierce the backs of our prepubescent noggins. It was during that time that hair teasing was hugely popular, and I, needing *something* to help me in the looks department, decided to give it a go. I never once considered how high my bobby-pinned doily—mandatory in the Catholic Church—would stand atop my loft of red, frizzy hair which pyramided my taller-than-every-boy-in-the-class, lanky body.

Why someone didn't save me from myself is anyone's guess.

Anyway, unbeknownst to me, Sister spotted my poofed mound from her organ bench perch and, as soon as the last note was pounded out, marched herself to the back of my head and, making circular motions, ground her pointed fingernail into my skull, enlarging the circumference with each merciless twist. A Black and Decker power drill couldn't have done more damage. What hurt more than anything, though, was that she chose this humiliating tactic in front of the only crowd I cared to please . . .

. . . the eighth-grade boys!

When I told my mother, she delicately suggested that I had not followed the rules, and so it was my own fault that I had upset "poor Sister Carlotta." I guess had "poor Sister Carlotta" vaulted me from the choir loft to my death below, that would be my fault too. And I probably would have been in even more trouble for disrupting some old soul's funeral.

Not to mention—and much more importantly—I totally would have messed up my hair.

To my self-serving surprise, I wasn't the only one Sister targeted.

Glenn, my boy-crush, shimmied up a tree the April of our eighth-grade year and refused to disembark. (Get it? Dis-em-*bark*?) His defiance caused quite a commotion, but we all thought it bold and bossy and something that probably would get him tortured. The recess bell rang, but Glenn refused to give up his limb. I stood at the foot of the tree, gazing in awe at who I dreamed would be my future husband—this gutsy, valiant martyr willing to offer himself up sacrificially to protest how we were being persecuted.

Even though she had the right to be perturbed, Sister Carlotta displayed a dazzling lack of composure as she strutted across the playground to see what all the commotion was about. When she spotted Glenn, she declared—in no uncertain terms—that he needed to "Climb down from that tree right this minute!" He told her "No!" and his entire pack of supporters had the sense to avert their eyes and scamper to their classrooms.

I, however, would not scamper. I would stand by my man. Picture Romeo and Juliet. Bonnie and Clyde. Erin Brockovich and . . . well, whoever her neighbor-boyfriend was. (Of course, Brockovich didn't stand by her man, and he later attempted to extort money from her, but for a while they were really, really close.)

Poor Glenn. He was relentless in his efforts to put the nuns in a tailspin. Earlier that week, when footprints ended up on the boys' bathroom ceiling, the nuns didn't have to look far to find the culprit (although, to this day, Glenn denies his participation in the gymnastic feat). No one believed Glenn because, as a farm boy doing chores twice a day, he was the only one in our class strong enough to pull himself up and invert his body on the stall bar.

In hindsight, I think Sister Carlotta deserved credit for Glenn's overdeveloped biceps because she sometimes would discipline him by forcing him to stand with his arms outstretched while piling geography and literature books on top of his palms. For that, he probably should be thankful.

We would have gotten married except for one small thing: Glenn didn't know I existed. Which is ridiculous when you think about it since he and I had neighboring circles on the chalkboard. Whenever we were in trouble (pretty much, daily), Sister would point to our rings. Standing on our toes, we would press our noses into our assigned spots until Sister felt a tinge of mercy and released us from our torment. So, for Glenn not to feel a kindred spirit with me is preposterous, but because of that, I refuse to dwell any further on this not-so-isolated incidence of rejection.

Which is why the rest of this has absolutely nothing to do with Glenn. I've mentioned him a few times only so you can get a glimpse of the kind of persecution we endured during my elementary years at St. Mary's. My upcoming tale of woe is yet one more incident provoked when the nuns and priest ganged up on me.

At the end of each school year, an eighth-grade May Queen (trust me: it deserves a capital letter) was chosen to head up a celebrated, reverent church ceremony. Think Meghan Markle's wedding on a barnyard budget. The May Queen and her attendants would wear flowing, pastel, chiffon, and satin dresses with a flower headband supporting a short white veil. The church event, with its standing-room-only crowd, was the highlight of our highly academic, yet agonizing, eight years spent acting religious. From the time we entered St. Mary's School, all nine of us aspired to be the May Queen.

It was now our year, and the vote was taken. I had won! And yes, I voted for myself. It didn't matter that my mother couldn't afford that kind of dress. She could make me one, like she did my other non-hand-me-downs. What did matter was that I had somehow managed to beat all the other girls in my class! What were the odds!? Well, actually, one in nine.

I had been validated.

I mattered.

I was ecstatic . . .

. . . for about eighteen hours. That's when the parish priest proclaimed that a popular vote wasn't the best approach to select such a pious position. The choice would be made by the nuns and him. In the "one Mississippi" moment they took to discuss the matter, I was no longer the queen.

The decision was made. Chris, my first attendant, would become May Queen. And I . . . I wouldn't even be relegated to an attendant position. I had been ousted. Banished. Totally and completely rejected. Tena and Rita would be Chris's attendants, and I . . .

I would sit in the pew with my mother and watch.

Fine, I thought. *But I will tease my hair when I do.*

That ceremony was a sort of graduation for us eighth-graders. Apparently, our reputation as a group of hellions prevented even God from trying to coerce any nun to take us after that. We would soon be fed to the protestant junior high wolves.

Oh, happy days!

eight

A WASTE OF TASTE

It's okay if some people dislike you. Not everyone has good taste.
<small>ANONYMOUS</small>

How cool is that? I read it on a sign somewhere and thought it would make a pithy bumper sticker. Better yet, it would be a perfect life-slogan for these teens (actually, for anyone) who squander minutes/hours/days/months/years convinced they aren't enough.

So let's just pause right here and thank almighty God for bumper stickers. Amen and amen.

The pull to be validated by anyone other than God is a snare. Young girls, promised to be loved, can easily put their trust in someone who appears to have all the right answers, who baits their fragile egos with bogus compliments, who fills their gaps and appears to be whatever they are not. And before they know it, that person is controlling (subtly or overtly) their every move, and they are trapped. The ways of the world trump the ways of God.

Take an insecure girl who is desperate to be cared for, to be needed, to be valued, and add to that a hormonally charged boy who is bursting with desire for his immediate gratification, and the game is on. Only it's not a game. The U.S. out-of-wedlock pregnancy rate is proof.

Over 40 percent of all U.S. births are to single moms (compared to less than 5 percent in 1950), and each year 180,000 guys become teen dads. That equates to more than 1.5 million babies born into unmarried households, with only 20 percent of teen fathers marrying the baby's mother.[10] Unfortunately, approximately eight of ten teen fathers will end up flying the paternal coop, with most children born to teen dads never knowing their fathers. No surprises there. Most of these "dads" themselves grew up in a fatherless household.[11]

So how do we stop the ugly cycle? How do we convince young women that their value comes from their Creator and not from a hunk of burnin' love whose promises of caring for them almost always end up in the back seat of a car?

Someone once wrote, "Be careful whom you trust; the devil was once an angel." When we put our confidence in anything other than God, we risk failure. Pointing fingers at these overly testosteroned males is easy, but we need to remember that we all are born with an ugly heart, and all of us are capable of deception. Who of us hasn't pretended to be something we aren't? Who of us, for personal gain, hasn't flattered or manipulated or gossiped or _____? (You fill in the blank.)

The only time we aren't vulnerable is when we hope in God alone. Psalm 118:8 instructs us wisely: *It is better to trust in the Lord than to put confidence in man.* Isaiah 2:22 tells us why. *Don't put your trust in mere humans. They are as frail as breath.*

Yes they are.

Correction: yes we are.

If we learn to reaffirm who we are in Christ, our behavior will align with that belief, and we will begin to reflect our true identity in him. Get that? We are the temple of the Lord (1 Corinthians 3:16). Jesus is involved in where we go, with whom we hang, how we speak, what we wear, how we love. Basically, he's our lifeline, 24/7.

In John and Stasi Eldridge's book *Captivating*, Stasi writes, "I know I am not alone in this nagging sense of failing to measure up, a feeling of not being acceptable as a woman. Every woman I've ever met feels it—something deeper than just the sense of failing at what she does. An underlying, gut feeling of failing at who she is. *I am not enough, and I am too much at the same time.* Not pretty enough, not thin enough, not kind enough, not gracious enough, not disciplined enough. But too emotional, too needy, too sensitive, too strong, too opinionated, too messy. The result is shame, the universal companion of women. It haunts us, nipping at our heels, feeding on our *deepest fear that we will end up abandoned and alone.*"[12]

Stasi's words described my journey. It had taken me far too many years to figure out who I am in Christ. I mean, I would claim I wanted to know God better, yet my negative self-talk kept me from seeing Him as my loving Father who wanted me to know of my incredible value, who was desperate for me to bring all of my cares and concerns (including my inferiority) to Him, who made me with imperfections so I would not become my own idol, who disdains culture's definition of "success" but cares that I live a life of significance, who needs me to remember Who matters most. (Yes, I know that is an annoyingly long sentence, but it felt most truthful to write it that way.) If I could do that, I would have a head start on being confident in who I am. In loving myself. So that I would be free to love others instead of competing with them.

> I've never met anyone, except mature Christians, who "have it together," and the only reason they do is because they know who Christ is in them.

The same is true for you and for those young women in my Bible study. The truth is, I've never met anyone, except mature Christians, who "have it together," and the only reason they do is because they know who Christ is in them. It has nothing to do with their individual strengths or attributes or how many cupcakes they baked for the church social or how many years they toiled as missionaries in the African jungle. Nothing! They stopped fighting that battle long ago because they realized it was one they could not win.

Even the Bible, God's Word to us, is jam-packed with redeeming stories of "Who's Not Good Enough" individuals. Here's my short list:

Noah was a drunk.

Abraham was a liar.

Leah was unloved.

Moses was a stutterer, a murderer, and desperately insecure.

Joseph was a braggart.

Samson was a womanizer.

David was an adulterer and a pretty lousy father.

Rahab was a prostitute.

The apostles were disrespected misfits.

But here's the crazy cool part: God used all of them to be central figures in His grand story. Just like He wants to do with those young gals in my living room. My concern was valid. Would I be able to convince them to stop wasting so much time believing they weren't good enough?

I had no idea.

What I did know was they weren't the only high schoolers with hurting hearts. The assignment for my speech class juniors to create eulogies shortly after the second semester began was proof. Students were free to write a "goodbye" to anything that no longer remained in their life. Some chose humorous anecdotes: bidding farewell to their belief in Santa; losing their first tooth; crashing their tricycle; dismembering their Barbie while playing doctor; boxing up their GI Joe toys which were no longer cool, and more along these lines.

And then there were others, two copied here, verbatim. (Thus, the grammatical and spelling errors are purposely left.) The first was written by a beautiful, bright, gifted young lady who surprised the entire class with her confession.

A Goodbye Innocence

I remember being a little girl, lying in the grass, dreaming about my future . . . who I'd be . . . what I'd become. I'd meet a boy, no a man, and we'd fall in love, get married . . . and be happy. But not only that, I'd be beautiful, successful, someone people look up to! This was my dream. But as I grew older, I noticed I was slipping farther and farther away from me. What I wanted . . . what I dreamed of . . . I was destroying. So this is my goodbye to innocence, to childhood pleasures and dreams, and to everything I wish for badly . . . but can never have back.

I grew up without my father, just like many. His drugs, his women, and his lifestyle were more important to him than me. I remember seeing him hit my mother . . . after that we left. I've never had someone in my life to teach me what a "Daddy" is supposed to be. There is a man in my life . . . but not a "Dad." This man . . . not a day has gone by since he stepped in that he has let me forget what a worth less (fill in the blank) I am. I don't remember the first time he hit me . . . only that my heart hurt more than my face. That's probably when my dream of how peaceful, and innocent, and prosperous I would become left me. I was angry. I was bitter. I developed depression and anxiety by the third grade and it's something I've had to deal with since. It's not something that I can just . . . make go away or control, sometimes my emotions get the best of me, but I'm learning . . . just like the rest of you.

In the 8th grade my life came to a turning point. I could keep my innocence, keep dreaming, and learn to forgive, but I chose the other path. I began to cut myself and drink every night. At school I'd put on a smile and pretend it was all okay, then go home alone and drink my pain away with my parents vodka. Then came freshmen year. It got a little harder to maintain my stress-free drunken lifestyle. So . . . I turned to boys. After I lost my virginity to my first boyfriend, it became so easy to have sex with . . . whoever. It made me feel like I had some sort of control over my life when I made boys want me. When in all actuality, my addiction was controlling me. Now I could never be the pure wife I had wanted to be.

By sophomore year, my addictions were out of control. I was smoking weed and snorting the ground-up pills, and drunk cocktails my friends gave me, all to make the pain go away. There was a monster inside of me. I would do anything, ANYTHING to feel good . . . but it wasn't worth it. I can never have the time back I wasted. I can never have my innocence back, and I can never have my dream back.

Over last summer I was sent to what I call a "boarding school," but it was really a behavioral program where I learned a lot about myself and how to let go. But when I came home, I got back into my old life-style. I wanted SO BADLY to show everyone I was different but no one believed in me . . . how was I supposed to stay strong with no one holding me up? I'm learning now how to stay strong on my own . . . cause let's face it . . . it doesn't matter how many friends I have or how much support they give me, I always feel alone.

I now have heart problems due to the pills I've done. But the physical problems are NOTHING compared to the regret of what I've done. But now, it's not only time to forgive others, but myself. There's so much pressure from everyone around me to be perfect . . . and that's just not who I am. I know I've always been good at PRETENDING I'm comfortable with myself, but now, I actually am. I've accepted my past and forgiven myself. My innocence is gone and I can't have it back. But my past is gone too. I can't change it. But what I can do is look ahead to my future. My innocent dream is gone, but a new one has taken its place. And this dream . . . is to be happy.

The saddest eulogy was presented by a 17-year-old who sat in the back of the classroom, veiling her face with her long, stringy hair; she did everything to avoid attention. Her speech, below, also is reprinted exactly as she turned it in to me. So paralyzed was she to deliver this eulogy that she asked that Mrs. Kendrick, her art teacher and trusted friend, be permitted to sit in the front of the room as she spoke from the podium. Of course, I said yes.

Ode To Childhood

Disclaimer: This is the hardest thing I've ever had to do. Some of you will be shocked by this confession but I need to do this for myself.

Ah, childhood. Remember it? Playing outside until late dark? This was my life at 3. Wonderful, fun, lovingly, everything seemed great.

Until I turned 4 years old, everything shattered around me. As a child, I was molested and raped by a family member. I can still feel the shame he instilled in me. I was only 4, not old enough to understand that what this man whom I lovingly called "grandpa" was doing was wrong.

It started out normal enough, I was misbehaving. However instead of setting me in a corner like what he always did, he sent my sisters upstairs and asked me to stay where I was.

From then, weekend after weekend, I was tortured. Every time he sent my grandmother and mother to go shopping or every time he sent my father to work in the garage, it happened with a snap of his fingers. "It's a special love" he once told me, cleaning up the mess. Special love? What makes that love? As I remember love doesn't feel like shame, fear, and self-loathing. He said my own father would soon be doing this to me and that he was merely helping me overcome it.

My relationship with my father suffered after that.

I remember going to bed; bleeding and confused. But more so scared. Very scared. Not even a teddy bear's warmth could calm my nerves.

He beat my sister and called the other names because of her speaking difficulty. We never told our parents. Would they believe us?

Oh, mom. I wish I had told her. She asked us repeatedly if he had done anything inappropriate.

We lied.

I still can see the look in her eyes as I laid down beside her, scared over a nightmare. She asked me one last time. Did he do anything to you? I couldn't look at her. I couldn't speak. My mind scrambling for an answer. What do I say? She wouldn't believe! He said! He said!

We cried that night together. Broken and drowning in forgotten words. This is my least favorite memory.

I remember, he had a way of putting me down. Making me feel like scum. Worse than scum to be honest. I was in my 6th grade year and I wanted to be in the talent show. Why? I don't know, I just wanted to be able sing. I knew I wasn't as good as my classmates, but hey, I liked singing and wanted too. Was that such a crime?

According to him it was. He told me I was a horrible singer and that Id best give up that dream right then and there. He wanted me to be a dancer. That is why I don't dance or sing anymore.

I know what you're asking yourselves. Why didn't you tell anyone? Well, no matter how bad it got, I foolishly believed he'd change. Every night I prayed for this and I was broken when he gave that look.

That look . . . broke me. It sickens me to this day that I even thought I loved him as a family member.

The other day I saw a little girl. She had to have been five or sixish it looked like. I found myself wondering. What is her life like? Is there a bad man in her life? Does she feel like her whole world is slowly falling apart every time she looks at that bad man? Does her heart shatter and tear in little pieces . . . and no one can help her pick them up? Is there someone, anyone, willing to believe her?

This man . . . no IT . . . died when I was 13. I didn't tell my mother until last year. I am 17 years old now. I have a great boyfriend, a wonderful family, and perfect friends who love an support me. I am blessed. I'm now in therapy for treatment. Hopefully, this will heal my unseen wounds.

I want . . . to be me finally. I want to sing, I want to dance freely without his judgment. I want to do these things without sympathy. Without feeling tied down. Without the fear of falling.

So this is my ode to childhood and the man who killed it. An ode to my pain. I refuse to let this sorrow, this tragic event rule over me no longer will I be controlled by this. I refuse to live in the past and pray that the future will be worthwhile.

I never will forget that day. As this dear, sweet soul shared her pain, even the football players couldn't remain dry-eyed. Sitting in the back of the classroom to critique the speeches, I couldn't see my evaluation sheet because of tears falling on the page. As classmates sat stunned, Mrs. Kendrick and I moved from our seats to embrace this brave, young girl and tell her how proud of her we were. No one was unmoved. Her transparency opened everyone's eyes to hidden secrets.

Because of her realness, she had given her classmates permission to do likewise; none of us left that day unchanged. Requests poured in from my other students to rewrite what they had prepared, a request I knew might heal a lot of hurting teenage souls, souls who now would trust the rest of us with their realness.

Revisions included painful times or choices. The incarcerated father who never would walk his daughter (my student) down the aisle. The moment when a star football player was told his playing days were over because of a third concussion, a speech that left his best friend and the team quarterback kneeling and sobbing after class. Cutting. Alcohol and drugs. Separating from an abusive boyfriend. Middle school bullies. Coaches whose heartless actions left youngsters on benches.

To say these speeches were painful is an understatement, but what came from them was a sense of relief and a desire to move on, to no longer give those who had caused so much grief the power to destroy these students' futures. They were beginning the honest process of saying goodbye to the shame triggered by the wrongs made to them or by them.

I knew God was doing a miraculous work in their lives. Paul's words in his letter to the Philippians were being played out in my classroom: . . . *he who began a good work in you will carry it on to completion until the day of Christ Jesus.*[13] That Scripture was true for my students, just as it is true for you and me. We all must be steadfast in believing God's truth over our circumstances.

No doubt God was grieved over what these teens had endured, and now they were helping their classmates to see hope in their pain. Without realizing it, they were demonstrating the truth of 2 Corinthians 1:3: *Praise be to the God and Father of our Lord Jesus Christ, the Father of compassion and the God of all comfort, who comforts us in all our troubles, so that we can comfort those in any trouble with the comfort we ourselves receive from God.*

There was a renewed confidence in those who had braved to share their stories, so when my drama students—some who also presented eulogies—were asked to create and perform morality skits for the incoming freshmen, the task was not taken lightly. While brainstorming ideas for skits to address some of the problems teens were facing, I heard it all: alcohol, drugs, abuse, bullying, sex, anorexia, cutting, thoughts of suicide . . . you name it, my group lived it. Much of it was in the past, but unfortunately, some was in the present. And many of my students were Christians.

"How many times have you been *told* that these behaviors are destructive patterns that solve nothing?" I asked. They stared at me as if I had just fallen off the stupid truck. Words, my drama students knew, were not sufficient; we would have to be creative and "cool" to get these younger students to pay attention.

Therein was the problem.

How could we get those boys and girls to understand that, in spite of all the negativity surrounding them . . . parents who were absent or infused with their own behaviors of insecurity . . . classmates who make fun of them because of their clothes or hair or unsocial mannerisms . . . guilt over their physical ineptness or mental deficiency . . . they still were valuable? They mattered. And alcohol, drugs, and all of that were only temporary Band-Aids to mask their need to be appreciated, to be treasured.

After a spirited dialogue, I polled my students. "How many of you are not okay with yourselves right where you are?" Out of the twenty-six students in that class, all but one raised a hand. I watched them look around the room, stunned by what they saw. Classmates who were in the "in" crowd—those with incredible talents and awards, those who always had been admired—even their hands were raised. It resembled our Bible study poll, only on a grander scale.

Most of us are no different than my students. We give ourselves permission to feel inadequate when someone or something makes us feel inferior. My preschool years had much in common with the kindergartners my high school students interviewed. I was loved and delighted in and could morph from a princess to a tomboy pirate to a tap dancer (and be a star at whichever role I chose) depending on which neighbor or brother-playmate was lucky enough to befriend me that hour.

I was unbroken.

It was a confidence that did not last. The continued insensitivity of teachers and cruelty of classmates would soon indoctrinate me into society's pecking order. For goodness sakes, even my happy moments—albeit not as long-lasting as I desired—added to my inferiority complex. How was that possible? Read on.

nine

PAYBACK

You weren't made to fit in. You were born to stand out.
JIM CAVIEZEL

I laugh on the inhale. I have tried to laugh on the exhale, but it sounds desperate. My barking seal imitation, combining a wheezing snort and an asthma attack, provokes people to murmur, not to mention strongly dislike me, because I appear needy and attention-seeking, which, in this isolated case, is not the . . . well, case. Dave used to be embarrassed by my cackle until a waiter in a prestigious restaurant presented us with a bottle of champagne for bringing such joy to his customers when I got tickled and, one table at a time, all the patrons joined in. It was a *My Best Friend's Wedding*, Cameron Diaz-singing-karaoke moment.

Minus the whole beauty and talent part, of course.

Anyway, it should come as no surprise to anyone that ninth-grade teachers don't have the same sense of humor as clients in fine-dining establishments.

His name was Mr. Smith, and he was tall, good-looking, and patient when the fifteen of us St. Mary's transfers entered his ninth-grade public school classroom for the first time. We quickly learned that rules in junior high were much less restrictive than what we had encountered with our elementary, prisoner-of-war experience. For example, ever since first grade we were required to stand beside our desk when answering a question, but now when we rose from our seats and the public school kids snickered, Mr. Smith gently would tell us we could answer sitting down.

It felt irreverent.

Disrespectful.

Criminal.

But oh, so liberating.

Chris was now my best friend. I'm not sure why. She came from a middle-class family, never had to work after school or on weekends, manicured her fingernails nightly, constantly lotioned her freckleless skin, and had enough clothes to make it two weeks without wearing the same outfit. In later years she was nominated for football homecoming queen. I, on the other hand, hung streamers and blew up balloons to decorate the gym for the dance that followed . . . the dance I wouldn't attend unless a group of my other dateless girlfriends and I went together.

As the model student, Chris lived in fear a teacher would scold her, whereupon her mother, Mildred, hearing that her daughter wasn't perfect, would have a heart attack and die. (No hyperbole intended.)

Chris had an uncanny knack for whispering something funny to me when the teacher's back was turned and then professing innocence when I snorted and the teacher pivoted to find me with shoulders shaking and tears in my eyes. He would reprimand me in front of my classmates, totally ignoring the fact they also were cracking up because of me trying not to. Chris could have been Mother Teresa's double as a poster child for innocence. I'm sure that, had there been a May Queen in junior high, my saintly friend would have been chosen.

I, however, would have been sitting with my mother, watching the proceedings. Yes, with teased hair.

Anyway, within a few weeks of entering junior high, I was getting a reputation as a troublemaker. Not trouble as in threatening to stab someone or burning a teacher in effigy (although within a few years I lost my ability to brag about that effigy thing), but it was more like the talking and laughing kind of trouble. That's all. No biggie. What I appreciated about Mr. Smith was that he at least took me into the hall when he wanted to threaten me. So let's just pause right here and appreciate a man like that.

By the end of that school year, thanks to Chris, I had been forced to switch classes with three different teachers, educators who, in a small town like mine, never forget. Never. (Like eleventy billion times they had a chance to!) As you saintly types can't possibly know, there's nothing more awkward than running into former educators who, years after you left their classroom, used you as their example of how *not* to behave.

I should have learned my lesson concerning people I allowed to influence me, but I was born with an excess of naivete genes. Our sophomore year in high school, Chris talked me into taking debate. She had to push a couple of buttons, but when she found the right one, it was the red, nuclear control in the Oval Office of Argumentation.

"I hear we get to travel on Friday nights and stay in motels."

Not interested.

"And they give us a dollar-a-day meal money."

Hmmmph . . . I made that in two hours as a nurse's aide at the hospital.

"All kinds of cute guys are at the tournaments."

I sprinted to the office to sign up.

Even though my mother always claimed that there was no discussion about which I could not argue, I soon found out my motels/money/guys motivation did not qualify me to set the world of argumentation on fire. Actually, I would have settled for a spark.

It was the late sixties, and there were no copy machines or computers, nothing to help streamline the actual research we were required to do from books, newspapers, and magazines. All of our handwritten note cards of evidence were stowed in a 3-by-5 recipe card box.

At least that was the plan.

My tin container held few, if any, pieces of evidence. Mine was chock full of diary writings about names of boys I fantasized would ask me out. I think Chris's box held hand lotion and a mirror. Possibly lipstick. I certainly don't remember any actual research tucked away in either box, which makes me wonder what Chris and I were doing when we were assigned library duty. It was all I could do to memorize the national debate topic: "Resolved: That nuclear weapons should be controlled by an international organization." In case you're impressed, time for full disclosure:

This morning, I Googled it.

Regardless, the fateful day came when Chris and I were expected to debate in front of our classmates, ninth-through-twelfth graders, and for some reason, we were paired against Bob Farmer and Bob Eshelbrenner, the kingpins of the squad, seniors, owners of multiple trophies from the tournaments they attended and won. We were novices and . . . how shall I say this gently?

Pitiful.

The Bobs, representing the affirmative position and defending the resolution, sat at a table on one side of the room. Chris and I, the negative team, sat on the other. Bob E. stood, addressed the judge (our coach), our classmates, and us, his opponents, asking if we were ready. I made a mental note of how he started.

While Bob One spoke, it was our job to "flow," to write down whatever the affirmative said in a long, two-inch-wide column, and then script our arguments directly beside what our competitors said. I scribbled furiously, not wanting to miss anything of importance (which would have been more than helpful had I known the difference). Chris doodled notes to herself about how cute our challengers were and applied hand lotion.

When it was the negative's turn to speak, I turned to Chris and signaled for her to go first. She whispered something like "Over my dead body!" and that she "wasn't ready." She had "no idea what to do" and pointed to the fact that I actually had flowed and she hadn't. My life flashed before my eyes as I panicked and informed my partner, in no certain terms, that *I* sure didn't know what to say. Chris said that she didn't either, and she was not about to embarrass herself.

Like she had any idea what *that* meant. After all, she was gorgeous, dressed stylishly, boys sought her attention, and she smelled great. I guess she knew that since I lived in a world of humiliation, this would be no big deal. Also, any call home to her mother, Mildred, would be a death sentence. My poor mother was used to it.

There was no point looking into my file box and even less looking into Chris's. I stood. Walked to the tilted, oak casket podium and placed my flow on its leering ledge. Scanned the room. Faced the execution squad. And spoke.

"Judge ready?" Our coach nodded. He seemed pleased.

"Audience ready?" My classmates stared at me like I had just hypnotized them into a coma.

"Affirmative ready?" I never should have made eye contact. Picture starving crocodiles feasting on the carcass of some poor, innocent mama zebra who made the fatal mistake of simply lapping from the area lake when—*wham!*—she's turned into striped brisket. Their snarls told it all. What I was about to say might be the last words anyone ever heard from my zebra-ish lips.

"My colleague" —who nodded, smiled, and continued rubbing her sweet-smelling hands together—"and I . . . "

Insert long, long . . . loooonnnnng . . . pause.

" . . . disagree with everything the affirmative just said."

And holding my head up high as if sniffing the ceiling, I picked up my flow and coolly—maybe as cool as I ever fake-acted—strutted back to my chair.

Imagine my excitement when our coach tossed his head back and laughed uproariously. More thrilling was how the Bobs, appreciating our unique approach, crossed to our desks, shook our hands, and asked us for a date.

Yes, imagine all you want, but the truth is, that would be a lie, and you know . . . that bowels-of-hell curse thing . . .

Our coach—of that delightful old school of teachers who had no reason to fear the school board or the ACLU—went ballistic. His neck veins bulged like a bloated jellyfish, causing his face to turn crimson, and he began banging his clipboard on his table, screaming at us for being unprepared, that never in his lifetime of coaching debate had he "ever, ever heard anything so wretched."

Not even Sister Carlotta had shown that degree of aggression, so being relatively unfamiliar with this display of madness, I ignorantly assumed that our coach would run out of steam. Wrong. Had he a knife and not a clipboard, Chris and I might have become the dartboard for his hostility. For goodness sakes, it wasn't like we were intentional in our incompetence. Surely our coach could tell the difference.

Besides, this was all Chris's fault. She's the one who talked me into this activity. For perhaps the first time ever, this was not my doing. (May I tell you how glorious it feels to say that?)

In any event, with the exception of my partner, "we" sat motionless, fearing for our lives. Chris hastily hid her lotion in her recipe box and took on that same look she used multiple times in our junior high escapades. Pointless. Verbal attacks flew like nuclear warheads as the two of us were the recipients of a tongue-lashing of cosmic proportions. How times have changed: had that happened to me today and some empathetic classmate chanced to catch a video of it, Gloria Allred would be standing beside me on the steps of the Capitol.

Too bad it was 1966.

At the end of the year, Chris dropped out of debate. For some reason, probably the future husband I might meet, I hung in there. Honestly, I have no idea why. That being said, debate ended up being life-changing for me, and even though I never dated any guys because of it, doors opened for me that I didn't know existed. My motivation to participate, as pathetic as it was at first, paid off. I found that I could think as well as argue, and success in the form of a college debate scholarship followed.

And when I became a debate coach several decades later, it gave me a wonderful motto to share with my terrified, unprepared, novice debaters: "I've never learned a lot from winning, but I've learned a doozy of a lot from failing."

As for those junior high teachers who used me as a bad example, I am pleased to announce that I had the last word. Literally. Decades later, as a public speaker, I had an opportunity to address a group of retired teachers. In that audience were two of the former educators who had kicked me out of their classes for talking too much. *Ironic*, I told myself. *One day I'm booted for talking, and today, they pay to hear what I have to say.*

Sometimes justice is sweet!

ten

FIRST, LAST . . . LAST, FIRST

We all wear masks, and the time comes when we cannot
remove them without removing some of our own skin.
ANDRE BERTHIAUME

The teens sitting in my living room are shocked when I say that seeking others' approval as a way of feeling validated can be a sin. But it's true. Should my motive be delighting in myself according to accolades I receive instead of bringing delight to others, there is a good chance I am sinning.

Proverbs 29:25 (NIV): *Fear of man will prove to be a snare, but whoever trusts in the Lord is kept safe.* Once we cherish what others say about us, once the receipt of praise becomes our motive, our moods are easily affected, and this is a grievous assault on how Jesus instructed us to live. The message to God is egregious: *Your opinion of me is not as important as the people I care to impress.* We fight Him for His throne and decide our idea of reality is more valid than His. We fail to honestly evaluate our standing. As my dear friend Carol once put it, "What's good is God, and the rest is

> The message to God is egregious: *Your opinion of me is not as important as the people I care to impress.*

me." Perhaps if we could grasp that truth, we would know what matters most. We would step aside and focus more on our Creator than ourselves.

The time had come for Jesus to find out who his disciples thought he was. Dr. Luke, who penned more of the New Testament than any other author, documented Jesus' words in Luke 9:23-25 (NIV):

> *"Whoever wants to be my disciple must deny themselves and take up their cross daily and follow me. For whoever wants to save their life will lose it, but whoever loses their life for me will save it. What good is it for someone to gain the whole world, and yet lose or forfeit their very self?"*

There it is. We are to take up our cross, not our crown, and follow the model Jesus established for us. We are to live humbly, not haughtily. Believing we deserve to be noticed or recognized or approved by others is not the way of the cross. So why do we spend so much time trying to figure out where we stand in the boxing arena of comparisons?

Here is the ring of combat: in one corner we have the world telling us that we are successful when others praise our strengths. In the opposite corner stands Jesus who says that we are successful when we surrender, when we are mindful of our position of humility instead of haughtiness, when we think of others before ourselves.

The difference is amply played out in Luke 18:9-14 where we read a parable about two men, a Pharisee and a tax collector, who went to the temple to pray. Standing alone, the Pharisee prayed: *"God, I thank you that I am not like other people—robbers, evildoers, adulterers—or even like this tax collector. I fast twice a week and give a tenth of all I get."*

The tax collector stood at a distance. Refusing to look to Heaven, he beat his breast and said, "God have mercy on me, a sinner."

Jesus explains in which corner of the ring he resides. *"I tell you that this man, rather than the other, went home justified before God. For all those who exalt themselves will be humbled, and those who humble themselves will be exalted."*

Can I hear an Amen?

When I read this Scripture, I realize how much God is not concerned with what others think or say about me. He is not impressed with my IQ or my designer wardrobe (if I even had one) or my volunteering at the homeless shelter or my life in professional baseball. He never asked for any of that to define me. He wants me to glorify Him. Period. Just like His son, Jesus, did.

Jesus was the model of meekness. Look whom he chose as his closest friends. For the most part, they were an uneducated mess: the ones bullied in school, the kind of chums who would make your parents' eyes roll if you brought them home for dinner. The unimpressive, the lowest on society's rungs of importance.

No doubt all of the disciples' résumés would have shown weakness. Did they stay that insignificant? Absolutely not. Following Jesus' resurrection, the Holy Spirit transformed their lives. They were molded into Christlikeness, and as you read Scripture, you never see them caring about how they fared in relation to the elites of their society. They were all about doing Heaven's work on earth no matter how much they were ridiculed. Even if it cost them their lives.

Which, for most of them, it did.

I know what you're thinking. Yes, it's hard not to be at least a little impressed with ourselves when we haven't screwed things up too badly, when everyone seems to be enjoying and appreciating us, but Heaven help us when our spouse or our boss or even a stranger seeks to destroy our self-worth.

If our goal is to get the approval of others or to try to be somebody we

> If our goal is to get the approval of others or to try to be somebody we admire, God will never hold His rightful place in our lives. We are serving the creation, not the Creator.

admire, God will never hold His rightful place in our lives. We are serving the creation, not the Creator, and when the approval of others becomes our ultimate goal, it will never be enough. Never!

People, people, people! If we live not to be rejected, we will forfeit the chance to fit into Jesus' depiction of what he looks for in a disciple, regardless of how the world presses in to have its way, bombarding us with ideas that others' opinions dictate our worth. Tragically, there is an arrogance in thinking that we deserve to be valued by man because true worth comes when we are humbled and unconcerned about everything other than being valued by God.

Jesus, our model of doing it right, left perfection to come to earth to be hated. Born in a smelly feeding trough to parents who couldn't even afford the required sacrifice of a lamb but offered two birds instead, Jesus' entrance to earth represented nothing like the Precious Moments manger scenes we display at Christmastime. And that was just the dirty beginning where it all started. The earthly end, the bloody crucifixion, was even more humbling.

The message of seeking the cross and not the crown is just as true for us as it was when Paul wrote his first letter to the Corinthians. From The Message version (1:27-31): *Isn't it obvious that God deliberately chose men and women that the culture overlooks and exploits and abuses, chose these "nobodies" to expose the hollow pretensions of the "somebodies"? That makes it quite clear that none of you can get by with blowing your own horn before God. Everything that we have— right thinking and right living, a clean slate and a fresh start—comes from God by way of Jesus Christ. That's why we have the saying, "If you're going to blow a horn, blow a trumpet for God."*

So there it is. We should be *all about* God and not ourselves. Our choice basically comes down to two things: the cross or the crown. Our human inclination would always be the crown, but that arrogance cannot win if we are followers of Christ. Eternal life has to trump whatever we fight for on this earth: power, prosperity, popularity, all the motives that can lead to pride and not meekness. Winning without Christ is still losing.

🏆 🏆 🏆

Our first step, I explain to the girls in our Bible study, is to understand that we are the least. If we can master that—daily take up our cross and follow Jesus and no one else—we will find out what it is like to be first. First in what matters most . . . which comes by being least . . . which goes against everything society tells us matters and everything these girls have believed. They have bought into the lie that they deserve to be different than they are (i.e., like somebody else), not realizing that that mindset is a sin. It completely lacks humility, and this is a dangerous place to be. In Francis Chan's book *Letters to the Church* he writes, "The most humble people are typically the happiest."[14] I agree.

If these teens are going to spend their adulthood with a sense of adventure and not regret, they need to stop wasting their lives trying to please others and accept that there always, always will be someone who will tell them they aren't good enough, and comparing themselves to others in hopes of affirming themselves is not the way of the crown.

Amen and amen.

I return to Luke with my girls giving their attention . . .

Jesus shared with his disciples about the literal cross he would endure. A fight broke out over who would be numero uno in Heaven. How Jesus didn't grab his friends by their throats is crazy impressive. He can't make it much clearer: . . . *"it is the one who is the least among you all who is the greatest"* (9:48).

The teens listen intently as I read from some scribbled notes: "If we live with the goal not to be rejected, if that is our motive for how we look, what we say, and what actions we take, we will not fit into Jesus' description of what a Christ-follower is like. This is a serious message with serious consequences for anyone with a serious desire to seriously matter."

Instead of trying to control others' opinions, these girls must decide whose opinion matters.

Instead of investing in impressing others, they must invest in what God desires for their lives.

Instead of seeking the crown, they must seek the cross.

And so must we all.

In *The End of Me*, author Kyle Idleman wrote about choices we all make. "In the kingdom economy, a lot is determined by the audience you choose. If you're most interested in what other people think, then their applause or attention is your reward. If they say you're a tremendous human being, then that's your reward. You've been paid in full, and you shouldn't look for any further commendation from God.

"But coming to the end of me means I am through with that charade and the emptiness of it. Instead, I seek only to please God—I receive my reward from Him instead of from people. When we close the public theater, drop the curtains, shut off the lights, and play to an audience of one, not caring about the reviews of the critics or anyone else, that's when we come to the end of ourselves and experience God's blessing."[15]

My brother David was an extraordinarily selfless Christian teacher and coach. To this day, fourteen years after his tragic death in a chain saw accident, his name continually emerges as one who changed lives for the better. He believed in each student he taught, even if they did not believe in themselves. David made people accept that they were special. Students and athletes alike shared stories of his confidence in their abilities. After David's November death, the school administration cleaned out his desk and found 163 Christmas letters he had written ahead of time to his students, each one personal and encouraging.

When I went into the grocery store a few weeks after his funeral, a toothless cashier told me how beautiful David always made her feel. I certainly didn't do that. I was always in too big of a hurry to recognize the potential in the woman scanning my groceries.

No more.

I began to see my students—okay, most of them—as a blessing. As insecure, questioning young men and women who needed to know they mattered. Regardless of what defensive walls they had constructed around them or the arrogant demeanor used to cover their insecurities, I now knew the importance of treating them with value.

Some made it harder than others.

Three years before I retired from teaching, I had a young woman in my speech class who made it known she absolutely hated speech; when I refused to accept her excuse for an assignment not turned in, she was livid. She wanted a B but was earning a C, and I held her accountable.

This bitter, unsocial senior was unashamedly vocal about her disdain for the requirements of the class and not afraid to show her attitude toward it (and me) whenever she could. Because of my brother's example, I tried to dignify her challenges with humor, silence, or a kind word. During the time when my students were delivering their eulogies, this young woman chose to speak on how her mother had abandoned her several years before and would not be coming to her graduation. There would be no party, no fanfare. She choked on her words as she delivered her speech.

It broke my heart.

But it also gave me a great idea.

What if we, her speech class, were to throw her a surprise graduation party?

The next day this young lady was absent, so I had an opportunity to run my idea by the class. They were as excited as I was. Each student was to bring a gift that cost no more than a dollar; I would bring the cake and punch, and we would have a class party for this hurting young soul.

I cannot tell you the emotional healing that was done the day of our surprise graduation party. It was one of the highlights of my teaching career. We pulled it off. I'm not sure who shed more tears . . . me, the rest of the class, or the senior. Did she still get a C? Yes. But her heart had changed, and she was able to accept responsibility for her irresponsibility. More importantly, she knew that she mattered. She left class that day beaming. So did everyone else.

Every teacher has opportunities to make a difference in the lives of his or her students. I cherished those opportunities, so when Alicia entered my classroom one day and started with a compliment, I knew this was going to be a very, very good day.

"Mrs. LaRoche, I just want you to know you are my favorite teacher of all time."

Classes had ended, and I was packing up the papers I would grade that evening when she began sharing how wonderful I am. I laid down the papers, took a seat, and encouraged her to continue. It was early in the school year, and this dear child already recognized what an incredible person I was.

Hopefully she had more to share.

I would wait.

Earlier that day, when students had paired up for a theater activity, I had chosen Alicia as my partner. Had I not, some poor soul would have been stuck. Even though the day had just started, her body odor and bad breath repulsed her classmates. No one wanted to get close to this outcast. That was then. This was now. I knew the hygiene issue needed to be addressed, but this was not the time. This was all about me.

"Why, thank you, Alicia," I answered. "You have made my day. Is there anything else?"

As my new BFF turned to exit, she had one last thing to say. "Yeah, it's really weird. My older sister had you and said you were one of her least favorite teachers. Crazy, isn't it?"

And with that, she turned and walked out of my classroom.

I sat at my desk, dumbfounded, questioning why her sister had such a horrific experience with me. The sad thing was, I couldn't even remember who her sister was.

Maybe that was the problem. Or at least, part of it. The truth was, before my brother died, looking for ways to build up my students wasn't always the priority it should have been. One place that made that clear was the high school detention room of which I was in charge. When faculty members wrote up students for not following school rules, these little darlings spent up to an hour after school with me. They learned quickly this was a no-nonsense place. One afternoon a young man entered and immediately got quite a reaction from several others who had already signed in. Smirks. Shifty smiles. I knew it in my mind: *Trouble.*

After asking his name, I told him to pull up his pants since groin-level waistbands were not allowed in our school. My remark got quite a rise (yes, a pun) out of the rest of the "detainees" who chuckled at my nerve. When my new arrival sat beside his buddy, I explained that one empty seat was required between each student serving time. Instead of following orders, he mumbled the F word, and this elicited the snickering attention he craved.

Although I managed to stay dispassionate—"Wow, darlin'! You must like me an awful lot, because now I'm going to double your detention and you're going to be spending even more time with me. You're going to be back here again tomorrow as well as today. Bad decision on your part"—I was seething on the inside. My thoughts were more like, *You impertinent little thug. You'll regret ever showing me up like that!*

Granted, I actually could have said what I was thinking, further aggravating the situation, but I still have to question why my thoughts were so unloving. Why wasn't my immediate response to see this young man through Jesus' eyes? To recognize his apparent woundedness instead of being so self-absorbed and prideful? To see that we all have our journey, and his, so different than mine in many ways, still pointed to wanting to matter, to be significant, to be enough.

It became all about me making my point with no regard for what God would like to do in this poor boy's life. Understandably, my clever response only antagonized him more. He muttered two more profanities before I asked him to leave and wrote him up. Our administration, frustrated over his behavior and history of trouble, suspended him from school. He never came back.

Then there was Denver, a special education student assigned detention. Denver wreaked rejection, as if his sixteen years had dealt him a steady stream of knockout punches, and my heart ached for him. The day he entered my room I saw him as Jesus did. Denver brought no textbooks, claiming he had no outstanding assignments, an admission that normally would get a student sent back to his locker to find something to work on. I made an exception for Denver. I asked if he would do me a big favor and sort through my container of magic markers, map pencils, and crayons to check which were worth saving. At first embarrassed, he glanced around the room to see if others were laughing at such an elementary request. When he realized no one was interested in our conversation, he mumbled, "Yeah, whatever."

Denver took great pains to check my writing utensils one by one. At the end of the hour, he brought them to me in color-coordinated groups. He was so proud of himself—and I was proud of him. I told him so. The next day I saw Denver in the hallway. Deserting his friends, he walked over to me. "Hey, Mrs. LaRoche. You know what my favorite class is?" Not giving me a chance to guess, he said, "Detention." That apparently was true because Denver soon became a frequent flyer in my elite little club.

I saw Denver through Jesus' eyes. Could I have made him leave when he had nothing to do? You betcha. But Jesus intervened, and I'm so glad He did.

Little did I know that, by the end of the school term, Denver would be dead, the victim of a horrific motorcycle accident.

God-thoughts will always pull us toward God. Always.

With the first young man, I was not concerned that he leave detention better than when he came in. I actually didn't care about him at all. I cared only about the way I looked to other students. Did he deserve additional detention time? No question. But by not demonstrating love, I added one more bruise to a hurting soul's spirit.

I had to wonder if I had done something similar to Alicia's sister . . . whoever she was.

eleven

SEW WHAT?

Every time I thought I was being rejected from something good,
I was actually being re-directed to something better.
STEVE MARABOLI, *UNAPOLOGETICALLY YOU:*
REFLECTIONS ON LIFE AND THE HUMAN EXPERIENCE

When I was young my mother taught me to sew, a love that was lost as soon as I—and whoever else viewed my Singer creations—realized I was as likely to become a fashion designer as I was to become a horse jockey. Somewhere in junior high. Come to think of it, that's when I decided I was inept at whatever it was I was attempting. Sewing was no exception. On home-ec assignments I fell in love with my pinking shears and would end up with more remnants than actual ware, even though my teacher, Mrs. Douglas (bless her heart), would always try to find some redeeming quality in my designs.

"Patty, that's a most creative bib," she would say with a *Yippee!* sort of inflection to her compliment.

"Mrs. Douglas, this is an apron."

If there is any exaggeration here, it's only by a few inches. Most times, the best thing that came out of my labors were the scraps that were taken home and stored for the quilt I someday probably would not make.

God knows all about saving remnants—which would have made a fantastic story to share with my high school Bible study group had I thought about it at the time. But I didn't. So hopefully they are reading this book and will have what they learned reinforced because of what they are about to learn.

The Bible is chock full of examples of God using remnants: Noah and his family rescued from the flood; Lot's family fleeing Sodom; seven thousand prophets spared from Ahab and Jezebel's terror; the Israelites entering the Promised Land; some fifty thousand people returning to Judea to rebuild the temple; the disciples; and all those who chose to follow Jesus.

I love stories of remnants, of castaways, of rejects who take advantage of second chances. Probably because I am one. And so are you, if Jesus is your personal Lord. This, people, is good news. The remnant theme did not stop in the Old Testament. Paul wrote to the Romans that "at the present time there is a remnant chosen by grace."[16] We are all invited to be that remnant as we return from our rebellious ways, rededicate ourselves to God's service, and find our way home to a welcoming, grace-extending Father who loves, rescues, and redeems us.

Crazy, isn't it? God does the work. All we have to do is accept it and live accordingly even though we don't deserve the quality attention He pays us. How generous of Him! We don't have to be good enough or holy enough. God accepts us as we are, and then He gets to work. As my granddaughter Montana says, "His (God's) goodness will rub off on you . . . because that's just the Person He is."

How can we not love Someone who gives so much? For goodness sakes, He even left us with the Holy Spirit to help us understand how valued we are.

I remember apologizing the first time I read in Scripture that my body was the temple of the Lord. I was anything but fitting as a dwelling place for something holy, mainly because I suffered from too many "too manys." Too many distractions while praying. Too many excuses for repeated sins. Too many cinnamon rolls. Too many "I'm not in the mood"s for exercising. I was a temple of something, all right, but it seemed hopeless that it could be the Lord. In reality, I felt like a colossal failure when it came to living up to any spiritual, faith-filled expectations required to be an example of a holy life. That's because I struggled understanding the depth of God's love for me.

🏆 🏆 🏆

This week, the Bible study gals and I would examine Scripture in hopes that they could begin to grasp just how much they are loved by a mighty God. What a better place to start than King David's journals, the Scriptures we refer to as the Psalms, where David wrote not as one who had it together but as one who trusted that God was working inside him in spite of his flaws. David seemed to have the secret: you won't always do the right thing, you won't always be faithful in your walk (or in my case, your crawl), you won't ever read or pray enough, you won't conquer every threatening mountain, and you won't ever be what you aspire to be. Still, God is faithful to redeem you no matter how many frays extend from your tattered psyche.

We might nod and agree that, yes, God is not going to abandon us, but the majority of people I meet feel like, in a way, He has. They just don't measure up.

Women in particular.

For some reason they have created a spiritual tape measure that causes them to think more about their badness than God's goodness. Consequently, they feel they never can perform enough to receive God's blessings. King David understood the root of that lie. He knew that pleasing his Father had nothing to do with a designated spot for prayer or a set number of minutes devoted to trying to get God's attention, but that it was all about accepting his Father's passion to love on David right where he was. Just like He wanted to do with the teens I was addressing. Just like He wants to do with you and me. Yet far too many of us focus on our problems, our weaknesses, and our remnant status instead of looking at what our Creator wants to do with us. From the inside out.

Let's face it. We live in a world of unfulfilled dreams. Maybe because we are still trying to earn our parents' praise or a few compliments from our spouse or boss. Or maybe we have created a screwed-up mindset that tells us we are stuck. There's nothing more. We are as good as it gets. Or maybe we just settle—as someone's sidekick, as her background singer, as his punching bag. We watch life from the sidelines and refuse to do what it takes to get into the game.

So, so wrong.

When we ask Jesus to be our Lord, a new creation is born within us. The old nature is gone; the new nature—the God nature—takes root. And that's where the conflict occurs. God can't sin, yet He indwells us fleshly beings who do err, and when we allow that sinful nature to trump what God is trying to do, we live defeated Christian lives. Lives with no joy. Author Anne Lamott created a phrase for the kind of joy God desires for us: "the best makeup."[17]

Fortunately, hope is not lost, for our Heavenly father is a master at redirection, not rejection. When we feel we are disappointing Him, He is right there, working inside us to pull us toward victory. The key is that we must lean in His direction. We must never give up. We must come to understand how precious we are to our Heavenly Father. To repeat, we must allow our remnant status to be redeemed. We will never serve God to our full potential if we don't believe we have "full potential" capability. God sees us as gifted. He is a beaming Father when He thinks of our potential. How arrogant we are to negate God's view of us!

> God sees us as gifted. He is a beaming Father when He thinks of our potential. How arrogant we are to negate God's view of us!

The truth is, in these mortal bodies we will never have it together no matter how fast we spiritually tap-dance to impress—but God will. The answer isn't to get big; it's to get small. The only safe place for a vulnerable soul is at the feet of Jesus.

In Psalm 119:8 David cried out, *"Oh God, please don't give up on me."*

The shout-it-from-the-rooftop news? He won't. He can't. That's His promise: "I will never leave you nor forsake you."[18] Get that? *Never.* No matter how much we sin. Because His temple—our body—is not for rent or for sale. It's His permanent dwelling place.

Perhaps you have bought into the lies of others whose own "remnant" status has made you believe that you always will be an unredeemable castoff. You aren't what you know you were designed to be, and you don't know where you fit in the eternal scheme of things. Not to worry! God is thrilled to gather you in His loving arms as He tells you that you are His prize. You are a remnant chosen by His grace! You matter most to Him. (I'm giving you a standing ovation!)

Remember the parable of the lost sheep? The shepherd left ninety-nine of his flock and went looking for the prodigal sheep that decided to do its own thing. Once it was found, the shepherd placed the lamb on his shoulders, returned home, and did the happy dance.

In Luke 15:7, Luke uses Jesus' words as he draws the parallel to us turning back to God: *"I tell you that in the same way there will be more rejoicing in heaven over one sinner who repents than over ninety-nine righteous persons who do not need to repent."*

Let me say it again: you matter! *You* are the one God is pursuing. He has a purpose for you. Please believe it.

For we are God's handiwork, created in Christ Jesus to do good works, which God prepared in advance for us to do (Ephesians 2:10).

So don't you ever give up. No matter how many times you fail or feel insignificant . . .

Which, in my case, didn't end with a sewing machine.

When I was in my early twenties, like most wanna-be hippies on the planet, I took up macramé, knotting and twisting and adding beads to whatever hanging planter I could afford to buy. But soon I tired of macramé and my hobby-love turned to needlepoint, where I found an endless supply of designs for my creative prowess.

Starting out with small, intricate patterns, I developed artistic skills that especially impressed nursing home residents, and soon I was needle-pointing much grander designs. My ultimate masterpiece was an owl. Yes. An owl. Three feet high and framed in faux wood. How it didn't land in the Metropolitan Museum of Art is proof even curators make mistakes.

Creating it was simple. Deciding who would be the recipient of my craftsmanship was much more difficult. Finally, after laboring over this dilemma, I decided to give it to my older brother, Jim. Lucky, lucky guy! I could hardly wait for his birthday to arrive, and when it did, I was at his front door, owl in hand.

When he finally spoke, his stuttering was my first indication he was beside himself. I left his house that day thrilled with my choice of heir to such a fine work of art.

Years later, I was talking to my brother's friend who happened to mention that Jim was moving, and she was helping him clean out his closets. She was nearly hysterical as she described the incredible garbage he had collected and then said, "Would you believe this? He actually has a needle-pointed owl that someone made for him . . . the ugliest thing you could ever imagine."

"Er . . . would that owl happen to be brown, with gold eyes, about three-feet high?" I asked.

"You've seen it? Isn't it horrible? Somebody gave it to him, but he can't remember who. Like someone's going to hang *that* in their house."

In case you're hoping I fessed up, I did.

Kidding.

Instead, I mentioned that I probably could find someone who would want it, and that I'd take it off my brother's hands.

As it turned out, my discriminating mother thought it was priceless. So endeared to it was she that she hung it in her spare bedroom, the one that held her fake poinsettia Christmas decorations, fur ball-laden spare blankets, and clothes destined for the Salvation Army.

Too bad my brother didn't inherit from our mother the same ability to recognize invaluable treasures as I did. He missed the point behind the present. This wasn't merely an owl. This was a stroke of genius and, now that I think about it, a poignant reminder of how God sees me. My brother and his friend saw its imperfections, like how some of its yard strands lacked consistent tension and how its talons weren't uniform. I saw perfections. After all, I had created it, designing it exactly as I saw fit: flawless, beautiful, my own hand's work of art. It took me decades before I understood that God saw me in the same way.

Receiving accolades from others should never be our ambition. I'm embarrassed to say that far too much of my life was spent with that end result in mind. Not surprisingly, as I have learned in my senior years, most attempts to seek lasting self-worth, self-acceptance, or self-confidence are self-defeating—until, that is, we learn to *whom* we need to look for our value. In other words, to repeat Diane's words, our desire needs to be Godfidence—and nothing more.

In his Sermon on the Mount, Jesus stunned his audience with these words: *"Blessed are the poor in spirit, for theirs is the kingdom of heaven"* (Matthew 5:3).

When have you ever equated anything "poor" with a personal objective? Certainly not on my bucket list. Who of us sees a street beggar and wishes to change places with him or her? Being poor runs counter to all we are taught from the time we are little. "Get a great education so you can have a great job so you can retire early so you can relax and live off of your investments." That's society's message.

It certainly isn't God's.

Granted, Jesus isn't talking about being monetarily broke; he's telling his listeners that their spirits need to be broken. There should be no drive for personal status or prestige or compliments. Those are worldly goals, not God's.

One of the most beautiful "poor in spirit" stories in Scripture presents a stunning contrast between society's dignitaries and its castoffs. Let's pick up the story in Luke 7 when Simon, a Pharisee, invited Jesus to his home for dinner. No doubt this man was a big shot in the community who loved to brag about his Sinai Club membership and his Cadillac camel—the one with the "Honk if you obey Yahweh" humper sticker pasted to its saddle—parked out front.

Things are about to get interesting. Jesus had been invited to the "other side of the tracks."

So snooty was this host that he failed to follow Jewish rules of hospitality. He did not wash his guest's feet, kiss him, or put oil on his head. One has to wonder if Simon's motive was to interrogate Jesus to trap him in an effort to esteem himself with the other religious leaders.

Enter the party-crasher, an uninvited, classless woman (many theologians say she was a prostitute) no doubt provoking stares and whispers as she walked directly to where Jesus was reclining and, weeping, washed Jesus' dirty feet with her tears. Let's stop for a moment. This woman wasn't a little weepy. She was gushing tears of passion as she subjected herself to even more ridicule by tending to her teacher, her Rabbi, her friend.

With no consideration for Jewish law which forbade women from letting down their hair in public, she did just that, drying Jesus' tear-drenched feet with her long tresses before she kissed them and anointed them with perfume. To the honorable dinner guests, this risky act was more than disdainful. Can't you just hear the gasps? The sinful woman didn't care less. She had one motive, and that was to bless her Lord. No matter how she appeared to the ruling class.

Poor in spirit? You betcha.

Then there's Snobby Simon. His thoughts are recorded in verse 39. *"If Jesus is a prophet as has been said, he would know the woman is a sinner and would not let her touch him and make him 'unclean.'"* It's an aha! moment for the host: *I've caught him now. He obviously is no prophet and he has violated Jewish law. Mission accomplished. Time for the cognac and fine cigars!* (And yes, the latter section is my interpretation.)

But before Simon spoke, Jesus stymied the crowd. Instead of defending the woman's heart, he shared a little story with his host: a money-lender forgave the debts two men owed him. One debt was large, the other small. Jesus asked Simon which debtor loved the lender more. A no-brainer for such an academic whiz. The Pharisee answered that the one forgiven more loved the lender more. Jesus agreed.

Looking for a thumbs-up from the guests, the chest of Simon's tunic was ready to burst at the seams. Then, not surprisingly, the tables turned. Jesus explained that the parable demonstrated why the sinful woman loved Jesus more—because she had been forgiven more. Simon failed to recognize he needed forgiveness. In so doing, he failed to love Jesus.

Slick Simon wasn't so cunning after all. His arrogance had publicly been trumped by a remnant, someone "poor in spirit," a prostitute no less. But here's the tragic part: we are given no evidence that Simon gets it! He had front row seats to a life-changing lesson—the same opportunity Jesus offers us—and he failed the test. Jesus recognizes love that is sincere and heartfelt. It reveals itself by admitting it needs forgiveness and is willing to be humbled—to the point of being publicly scorned (or even have an owl rejected), if that's what it takes—to prove it.

The tearful party crasher was flawed, deeply scarred, a castoff. Within a few hours she would go back to life as usual, but this time as one saved in a remnant, and filled with grace.

Maybe it's time we figure out that's not such a bad place to be.

I am proof that God can even use a remnant of inadequacy for his purposes.

It was my second time to speak in public. My home church in Texas had asked me to lead their ladies' Bible studies. The first talk had gone well, and with that nudge of confidence, I decided to be a little bolder in my next talk, possibly even use a visual or two.

My dear friend Cathy Tanana had told me of a lesson she had created to demonstrate the hierarchy of godly authority and protection by drawing umbrellas on the chalkboard, each one increasing in its diameter as it got closer to the top. She labeled the bottom, smallest umbrella as "children." Directly over that was "mother," her umbrella slightly larger than the "children" one. Father's umbrella was above it and even larger, Jesus' above that, and God's was the widest—everyone fit under God's umbrella.

I got to thinking: *Couldn't I do this even better? What if I had women hold actual umbrellas? Yes, that was it . . . brilliant!* I immediately went shopping, scouring for five umbrellas in various sizes and colors. I practiced my talk in the mirror eleventy billion times, praying my audience would become totally engaged, laugh or cry appropriately, and submit my visual to *Christianity Today*.

Upon arrival at the Bible study, Lael, the pastor's wife and friend who convinced me I could handle this, was excited to reveal that some furloughed missionaries would be there that day.

Not. Good. News.

My mind started whirling: *Missionaries know EVERYTHING— what can I possibly share with them that they don't already know? My lesson is engaging, but it isn't THAT engaging. Hopefully my umbrella analogy will save me. After all, they've never seen that illustration . . . since I made it up.*

Sort of.

Sweat began to frizz my hair. Oh well; the missionaries had come in from the jungle. Surely they had listened to speakers with bad hair days before.

I began by assigning parasol parts: Jana was the child; Linda, the mother; Vivien, the father; Jean was Jesus; and Pam was God. Pam thought that was swell; she said it was the first time everyone would have to listen to her. I reminded her that she was not to talk, even if she was God. She was just to follow directions and not screw things up; after all, the holy missionaries were there, and it was important they saw how Jesus lived in my heart, that he was my Lord and Savior, and that through him I could do anything.

Uh-huh . . .

Jana was up first, holding her umbrella high, directly above her head. I explained to the ladies that this was the child, and the child's first line of authority was the woman.

Which, as you probably figured out long before I did, presented a very real problem. Linda's umbrella had a handle (duh!) which, of course, prevented it from just sitting atop Jana's umbrella. Linda had to stand on a chair so her umbrella would "fit" over the smaller child's umbrella.

You're seeing this, aren't you? I was FA-REAKING out! *How in tarnation am I supposed to put the dad's umbrella over the mom's— suspend Vivien from the ceiling? And who knows where Jesus and God are supposed to go—ON THE ROOF?* It was a disaster. Women were staring at me with scrunched-up faces.

Cathy's umbrellas had been drawings absent the handles—a minor detail I failed to notice when I came up with my pathetically flawed lesson plan. By the time Vivien was trying to stretch high above Linda, the room was spinning. The women in the audience were trying desperately not to laugh, and I couldn't even look at the missionaries; they had to be glaring at me like I was a frizzy-haired, blooming idiot.

Never, ever would I speak again. I wanted to dig a hole and tunnel my way home, but what happened after the final "Amen" was the real shocker. While I was packing up my umbrellas and looking for an escape route, the "senior" missionary, the one who had been on foreign soil the longest, approached and asked if we could talk. I figured I was in for a spiritual tongue-thrashing on preparedness . . . or incompetence . . . or, deservedly, both. Then again, perhaps she just wanted to recommend her hairdresser.

What she said was anything but.

"I want you to know that was the best Bible study I've ever attended," she began. *Poor thing has been in the rain forest too long*, I told myself. "Well then, you've attended some pretty lousy Bible studies," I laughed. She dismissed my cavalier remark and continued. "Do you have any idea how many tea-and-doily Bible studies I attend? I get so tired of every speaker being so perfect, having it all together, and I can never relate to anything they say. The life of the missionary is extremely difficult, and we mess up all the time. I can't tell you what a blessing it was to see you mess up this teaching and be real."

I wanted to hug her, or better yet and much less offensive, offer her a choice of umbrellas.

Not surprisingly, that day I learned far more than the missionaries did. Being perfect is not a requirement to be used by God. In reality the opposite is true, and if that is the case, I realized I had plenty to offer. I left the church that morning dumbfounded. Was it really true that I didn't have to be near perfect—or even "okay"—to be effective for God? Could the opposite be true? Could it be that the less perfect I was, the more I could relate to other hurting souls? If so, I should be an expert!

> I wanted to hug her, or better yet and much less offensive, offer her a choice of umbrellas.

Are you seeing some patterns here? There was always, always something that caused me not to measure up, including my Christian walk. What must God think of someone who spent so many years suffocating in a performance trap instead of understanding the freedom she has as the daughter of a King? Even today I waste my time when I focus on my remnant status instead of God's grace-filled blessings in how I was designed.

I might label myself as a failure (self-recrimination is always *soooo* helpful; sarcasm intended), but my eternal Father never would. Get that? Never. He created me. He adores me. He forgives me. He wants me to be His representative, sharing with the world how He can take someone as unworthy as I am and use me for His kingdom's work.

Just like He desired to use the girls sitting in my living room.

Just like He desires to use you.

twelve

THE DISEASE TO PLEASE

I am not who you think I am. I am not who I think I am.
I am who I think you think I am.
REFLECTED APPRAISAL THEORY

AAARRRRGGGHHHHH!!!! This theory, proposed by Charles Horton Cooley, and taught in my speech class, was proving true in the lives of my Bible study group. Four weeks in, we are progressing slower than I desire. Last week's magazine assignment failed to perform the miracle I had intended. This week, I find myself praying:

Thank you, Jesus, that I am no longer a teenage girl. I do not miss the zits, gargantuan feet, body odor, unibrow, and desperation to be complimented.

I am close to an outbreak of psoriasis trying to impart a few nuggets of wisdom to these girls. Their negative view of themselves must be corrected if they are to enter adulthood with a renewed sense of their worth. Can I say something that will stop them from wasting the rest of their lives trying to please others, knowing that there will always, always be someone who will tell them they aren't good enough and that comparing themselves to others is not God's best?

I have no clue.

Especially since there seems to be an epidemic of watchdogs who believe they've been placed on this planet to point out the flaws of others. Take, for instance, my friend Juliette's tale. As she waited her turn at the punch bowl of a private party's fancy-schmancy oyster bar in Maine, a stranger walked up and gawked at her face, using the same intensity one would engage in while tweezing a chin hair. When Juliette asked if something was wrong, Ms. Hoity Toity Nasty had this to say:

"Did you know your eyebrows are supposed to be twins? Yours look like sisters, not twins."

At which point Juliette used her perfectly manicured acrylic nails to pull out the woman's tongue.

No, she didn't, but yes, I think it's possible such an action crossed her mind. What she did was nothing. She just stood there, stunned.

Upon hearing this account, my first reaction was to crack up, but it wasn't Juliette's, so I tried really, really hard to act mature and empathize as she told me what happened. (Still, I must admit I enjoyed this story, mainly because the negative focus was on someone other than me.)

Let me be clear. Juliette is stunning. She walks into a room and all eyes—and eyebrows— focus on her. With six-foot legs from her ankles to her sculptured cheekbones and a Julia Roberts smile, not to mention a sense of impeccable style, she draws attention. Typically, not this kind of attention. This is the kind of attention I typically draw, although I'm sure Eyebrow Lady would have contended that my eyebrows aren't even related and probably resemble an EKG print in full-fledged arrhythmia.

This obviously was a case of jealousy. Eyebrow Lady's way of making herself feel validated. Fortunately, Juliette knows who she is in Christ. She knows that God's opinion needs to be the only one that shapes her self-perception regardless of the shape of her eyebrows.

Which, let's be perfectly clear, are professionally micro-bladed and flawless.

Put yourself in Juliette's eyebrows. How would you have reacted? Would you have bolted to the bathroom or your car? Would you have simply considered the source and dismissed it? Or would you have poked Eyebrow Lady's eyes out? Most people, I'm sad to say, would be wounded by such an encounter. They would permit the eyebrow evaluator to ruin their evening . . . and perhaps the next few years of their life.

🏆 🏆 🏆

As they squeeze into cozy places around my living room, I look around our circle at the beautiful faces of these young gals who are rightfully well-known for their successes. I get specific and remind them of their athletic feats, their vocal contest ribbons, their honor roll status, their reputations, the way they have overcome difficult home lives. They feign listening. My attempts to build them up are bouncing off their hardened self-images like missiles off the deflector shields of the *Starship Enterprise.*

Switching tactics, I question if the girls know any classmates who have it together. They quickly name girls sitting beside them in my living room. The selected ones react like they have just opened their front doors to the Publishers Clearing House crew. "What? That's nuts! Me? No way!"

They seemed shocked, although secretly delighted, by this revelation.

I now ask if they can recall specific situations that helped create their insecurities. (It would have been wiser to ask which situations did not cause their self-doubts.) From the time they wake up until the time they go to bed, they feel inadequate. Even walking the school hallways is stressful, for there they wonder if other students are mocking their gait, their bangs, their waistlines . . . putting them on popularity trial for everything from the way they hold their books to a wisp of unruly hair.

What the girls in my Bible study and the students in my classroom (and, if truth be told, most women) fail to realize is that when our adequacy, our completeness, comes from our looks or our performance or our circumstance, we will remain broken. We, alone, will never ever be enough. That's why even something as simple as walking from one class to another can provoke feelings of inadequacy.

This landmark on the journey to wholeness was one I too had to make. From homely to beauty queen contestant; from unpopular to friend of many; from poor girl to middle class . . . I knew, firsthand, that none of that mattered. Broken is still broken.

Spoiler alert: even for Christians.

Think of the power we award to others! Giving anyone other than God the right to define our worth can turn that person into our idol, clearly violating the First Commandment: "Thou shall have no other gods before me." Move God off His throne, and we are the ones who suffer.

Let's be honest. When things are running smoothly, when no one is criticizing our eyebrows, when we seem to be appreciated by most people, it's a great day indeed, but what happens when our spouse or our boss or even a stranger manages to damage our self-worth? If our goal is to be validated or to try to be somebody else whom we admire, God will be in competition.

> This tug-of-war pits our Creator against His creation, with us lining up against God as we join the side of whosever's approval we seek.

This tug-of-war pits our Creator against His creation, with us lining up against God as we join the side of whosever's approval we seek. And when their praises become our goal, it never will be enough. There always will be another tomorrow when we will start anew, seeking to please, and if that desire is not squelched, we will become addicted to pleasing people.

Consider the work of Harriet Braiker, author of *The Disease to Please*, who warns her readers of the seriousness of such behavior. She lists four traits consistent in these individuals. [19] Check the box(es) of any that describe you:

☐ 1. A tendency to take criticism personally

☐ 2. A constant fear of rejection

☐ 3. Difficulty in expressing your true feelings

☐ 4. A reluctance to say no even when you should

There was a time I would have checked all four of those boxes. Compare that to the apostle Paul, who would have no checks. Seriously! He used himself as an example of what we need to emulate. There's no lack of clarity with what he said:

> *Obviously, I'm not trying to be a people pleaser! No, I am trying to please God. If I were still trying to please people, I would not be Christ's servant* (Galatians 1:10, NLT).

Somber stuff. Can you make that claim? Read that last sentence again. His bragging had nothing to do with his writing skills or his past studies under Professor Gamaliel or his resolve to be tortured without complaining or his popularity or his eyebrows.

Paul had confidence because Jesus found him worthy and died in his (Paul's) place. The apostle was grafted onto the same life-limb to which we are instructed to attach ourselves. In John 15:5, 6 Jesus said, *"I am the vine; you are the branches. If you remain in me and I in you, you will bear much fruit; apart from me you can do nothing."* Every breath I have, every smile I share, every kind deed I do, every time I forgive, every incident when I give no credence to spiteful comments, it is because Jesus and I are partnered.

In Hebrews 12:1, 2, Paul clarifies how we continue that relationship. *Therefore, since we are surrounded by such a great cloud of witnesses, let us throw off everything that hinders and the sin that so easily entangles. And let us run with perseverance the race marked out for us, <u>fixing our eyes on Jesus</u>, the pioneer and perfecter of faith* (emphasis mine).

Notice a few important principles. We must rid ourselves of whatever causes us not to follow God passionately. That includes any idol we place above Him, including anyone or anything that distracts us from knowing how loved we are. Sadly, far too many times we are that idol. In some cases, we demand perfection, even though Paul's choice of words "entangles" should serve as a warning.

When Dave pitched for the California Angels in the late '70s, a young outfielder was traded to the team. His wife and newborn soon arrived. I'll call her Carol. Carol's entrance into the wives' waiting room following the opening day game was legendary. She was stunningly beautiful and trendy, dressing much more chic (is "chicer" a word?) than the rest of the wives. After meeting her, I introduced her to the other wives and arranged to sit with her the following evening. We hit it off.

Returning home from the ballpark a few days later, Dave told me that Carol's family needed a place to live while their newly purchased house was being renovated. I welcomed the addition. After all, Carol was special. Not only was she a head-turner, she was multitalented. From singing to playing the piano to dancing to being a competitive tennis player to loving Jesus, Carol was the full package.

Her giftedness was recognized by everyone.

Except Carol.

The evening of the first day she moved in was proof. While I waited with my infant son to leave for the ballpark, Carol descended the stairs looking like a movie goddess. A goddess starring in a tragedy. In her opinion, her striking outfit had struck out. Handing me her sleeping baby in his carry-seat, she returned upstairs to start over. A fuss that was repeated . . .

. . . three times.

With each new ensemble, I bolstered my compliments, but they were incapable of undoing whatever negatives had been given permission to determine her value. This scene was acted out daily, and with each tearful entry, Carol's mascara-dripping makeup needed to be reapplied. Needless to say, we didn't make it to the ballpark for the singing of the National Anthem. Instead, we made a grand entrance, with Carol being the recipient of ogles and admiration. Fans saw her beauty. Other wives did too. Her attempt at perfectionism was her attempt to mask tremendous insecurities. And even though, in her mind, she was never enough, she pretended well and fooled a lot of people.

Which, as we all know, is exhausting. Years later when Dave coached for the Chicago White Sox, one of the wives was off the charts when it came to perfectionism. She vacuumed her rug several times a day so the pattern remained visible at all times. Pillow cases were washed daily just in case a stray hair found a home there. Had she died, I am convinced there would have been no DNA sample anywhere in her home. And yes, in case you are curious, she had small children.

Poor things.

"Failure" was not in her vocabulary.

We had nothing in common.

I don't remember her ever paying a compliment to anyone else; she viewed all the other wives as a threat—no one could do it as well as her. Her perfectionism intimidated. In Robert S. McGee's ageless book *The Search for Significance,* we are warned against such tendencies: "Perfectionists often appear to be highly motivated, but their motivations usually come from a desperate attempt to avoid the low self-esteem they experience when they fail." [20]

We must allow ourselves the privilege of being imperfect. And if I may brag a little, it is one area in which I excel.

Perfectionists fail to recognize that there are no performance-based activities that impute righteousness to us. Isaiah 64:6 says our best efforts at self-righteousness are as filthy rags. We are to be focused on Christ alone as our sole reason for being acceptable to God. It is not Jesus PLUS our performance. It is Jesus. Period.

Paul shares his secret for allowing this to happen in his letter to the Colossians (2:8): *See to it that no one takes you captive through philosophy and empty deception, according to the tradition of men, according to the elementary principles of the world, rather than according to Christ.*

Paul doesn't stop there. Ask yourself the question he asks in Galatians 1:10: *For am I now seeking the favor of men, or of God? Or am I striving to please men? If I were still trying to please men, I would not be a bond-servant of Christ.* Notice there is no compromise in Paul's message. It's an either/or ultimatum.

Perfectionists are rarely happy. Their elusive goal merely disguises their inadequacy, a belief that happens when we become trapped in the snares created by Satan's web of lies. His skewed lines we cross lead us nowhere near Christ. Our number one enemy tells us we aren't . . . *enough.* Not true.

Because of what Christ has done for us, we are more than enough. More. Than. Enough. No matter what anyone says. No matter what we tell ourselves.

Another thing to unpack in that Hebrews 12 Scripture is Paul's caution about the "race marked out for us." In other words, God's assignments are individualized. Your race is not my race, and my race is not your race. We all have our own lanes. In an actual race, should we venture into someone else's lane and mess with our competition, we will be disqualified. If you don't believe me, check out the 2019 Kentucky Derby when Maximum Security, the first-place finisher, went back to his stable trophy-less because, as his jockey later said, he "lost his focus." He drifted into other another horse's lane and was disqualified.

Paul instructed us where we need to look. Notice Paul's phrase "fixing our eyes on Jesus." We have only one place to spotlight, and that is Jesus. Amen and Amen. Averting our eyes to see how well our competition is doing alters our goal of following our own path for what God has prepared for us. People, stay in your lane.

In 1 Samuel 18 we are given a glimpse of someone who shifts his focus . . . with disastrous results. For a little background, Saul (tall, good-looking, noble) was king of Israel. He was also present when David killed Goliath. As King Saul and his soldiers returned home, women came from all the neighboring towns to celebrate their victory with singing and dancing. Let's pick it up in verse seven where we are told what the women did next:

> *As they danced, they sang:*
> *"Saul has slain his thousands,*
> *and David his tens of thousands."*

Saul was ticked. *"They have credited David with tens of thousands,"* he thought, *"but me with only thousands. What more can he get but the kingdom?" And from that time on Saul kept a close eye* <u>*on David.*</u>" (emphasis mine).

Oops! King Saul, once chosen by God to rule the Israelites, once choosing to please his Heavenly Father, now looks at his competition instead of his Creator. Surely he knew better. Surely he knew the story of Lucifer's fall from Heaven—the starting point for the devastating effects of competition—when Lucifer began to compare himself to God and sought the glory belonging to God alone (sound familiar?). Why would Saul look anywhere other than to God?

Probably the same reason you and I look to other places.

Keeping our eyes on the heavenly prize prevents things from becoming unfocused. Years ago, when eight-track tapes (yes, I am old) were popular, I was asked to make several copies for a local Christian school. Using the original, I made my first copy. From that one, I made my second. About the fifth one, I decided to check the quality. You can predict what that fifth copy sounded like. The fifth was not nearly as clear as the first. With each one that I copied, there were more distortions. Once I started over and made each duplicate off of the master, all were equally clear.

The message is obvious. When we look to others and attempt to be what they are instead of looking only to the Perfect One, we miss our mark. We enter a race not intended for us. This runs so counter to what makes us tick.

> When we look to others and attempt to be what they are instead of looking only to the Perfect One, we miss our mark.

Not to mention, this is the nugget I need to share with the teens in my living room, these young ladies suffering from the achingly common notion that others have the right to invalidate or validate them. Not only that, but by using others as a benchmark for how we evaluate ourselves, we cannot help but operate out of jealousy when good things happen to those we know.

If they, and all of us, can wake up each morning understanding we have two choices—God's opinion or that of others—we might have a chance after all.

thirteen

DISHONORABLE INTENTIONS

Always be a first-rate version of yourself and
not a second-rate version of someone else.
LOU KENNEDY

When I was in high school, debaters were thought to be the "brain elite" of our school, so with that label I was considered "smart." Trust me, I never felt smart, but through sheer determination—along with the assuredness that there were a lot of other things I could have been called—I would, by golly, accept and live up to that standing.

About the same time I began to grow into my nose and stilt legs, I found mascara, I had reason to no longer pad my bra with toilet paper, and guys began asking me out. I finally was worth their time (gag). Continuing to work after school and on weekends, as well as full-time in the summers, I could afford to buy stylish clothes from the local dress shop—in cash, always cash.

In spite of all of that, I was always just one stupid decision away from ruining any hopes of using my brain to do something intelligent with my life.

"Today we are going to see how much you know about the state of Kansas."

My classmates groaned. Not on my academic radar, I assure you. Our teacher continued. "The education department in Kansas is concerned that students don't know enough about their home state and are asking you to take this test to determine if a Kansas history class should be added to the school requirements." My classmates and I were told that following the quiz we would exchange papers with a neighbor and grade them so we would immediately know how we had done.

Grumble. Grumble.

I remember little except being handed a multiple choice test of maybe fifty questions about Kansas. I didn't even know there were fifty facts about Kansas, much less four options for each query. Still, I was developing a reputation for being smart. I had to excel on this test. Had to. Otherwise, what else would I hinge my acceptability on? (And yes, I know smart people do not end a sentence with a preposition.)

Let's see, I thought, mentally foraging for what I did recall about my state. *There's Topeka, our capital, Dorothy and Toto, tornadoes, a fort in Fort Scott, and . . . and . . . and . . . Glenda, the good witch, and . . . and . . .*

Mensa applicants would have been stymied. "What city in Kansas has the highest altitude?" *Seriously?* Kansas is flat, and since Sunset Street—where we sledded each winter, not to mention where I had ended up under a car when my brother Jim bailed from the front of our sled—wasn't included, I was at a loss. Not helpful for someone who typically made As and Bs and needed that attribute to make herself feel a teeny-weeny bit important.

The rest of this account, as a now-Christian, is shamingly hard to admit. Please don't hate me for it.

When the test was over, I glanced at my girlfriend "Sheila" sitting next to me, leaned over, and whispered, "You make all of mine right, and I'll make all of yours right." (Never would have been a consideration, I assure you, had I been named the holy May Queen.) Then, to be extra cautious, I added, "Make most of them right. We don't want to be obvious."

I'm bossy like that.

Sheila nodded, and as the teacher read the questions and answers aloud, we wore out our erasers as we changed each other's answers. I had missed more than I had gotten right, with my friend not far behind. We handed in our papers, proud of how we had pulled one over on our teacher . . . and the state of Kansas, hoping that the powers that be would reconsider the need for another mandatory class on something we already had mastered.

About a month later, Sheila and I were called to the school office. There we were greeted by the superintendent, our principal, the head of the Kansas Department of Education, a Congressman and someone from our local newspaper, *The Fort Scott Tribune*. You see where this is going, don't you? As it turned out, we two had the highest grades in the entire state of Kansas on that idiotic test we had cheated on four weeks earlier.

We were given certificates and featured in the *Tribune*, where we both looked like we had been electrocuted but were trying to enjoy it. After shaking hands and hearing "congratulations" from the entire impressive group, Sheila and I returned to our class, swearing to each other we would never, ever tell anyone we had cheated.

Shakespeare had it right: "The mind of guilt is full of scorpions."

I kept my promise for more than forty years, and even though it's a tale I've not often repeated following that forty-year moratorium, now that I'm a senior citizen and my mother isn't alive to drag me to the priest and force me to confess my sins, I've shared it with others who need to understand the necessity of honesty. One such person is my granddaughter, Montana. Montana's mother, my daughter-in-law, Jenn, recently purchased the historic Tribune building in Fort Scott. As I toured the site with them, they pointed out a stack of newspaper-sized scrapbooks from the '60's that had been left behind. Sharing my story, I told them to keep a lookout for our photo on one of the pages.

Lo and behold! About a week later Montana texted me a picture of the two of us imposters with our certificates. I would show it here except Sheila probably kept her promise never to share our crime and, unlike me, has kept her vow of secrecy. Me on the other hand?

My memory is a gift that keeps on stinging.

I hope that you never were so desperate to "matter" that you cheated to maintain your reputation. I hope you never invented a lie to be somebody you aren't, which prevented more deserving people from getting their just reward. (Trust me, I want to eat scorpions just thinking about what I did.)

Seriously. Somewhere in Kansas were two teens who perhaps had nothing else in their arsenal of self-worth except their knowledge of their home state. I picture them laboring over books for fun, memorizing facts, proudly reciting new research to bored parents and classmates. While the other kids were out playing soccer or practicing their guitars or debating, these individuals were intent on knowing all there was to learn about the center of our country. And then the infamous day to shine arrives. One of them deserves to win. One of them will win. Like those National Spelling Bee homeschooled kids who have spent years tackling words I cannot even pronounce, a high schooler's moment to matter is here . . .

Except, that is, for two cheating sophomores at Fort Scott High School. (Seriously, will my tongue swell if I eat a scorpion?) Our poor competitor maybe missed—legitimately—only one more than we did with our double-dealing, dishonorable methods, but this poor guy/girl got no satisfaction, no applause, no accolades . . . you know, like the ones we did—but shouldn't have.

You see, that's what happens when we attempt to maintain our status by doing anything other than honoring God with the gifts with which He has blessed us. For some of us, we will go to any length to dignify talents with which we have not been blessed but that give us even a modicum of notoriety. Perhaps it's our intelligence or our youthful sex appeal or our athleticism or our leadership ability or our creativity or our prayer life or (you fill in the blank.) After all, we have staked our reputations on that label and people have come to recognize us that way, so we will sacrifice just about anything rather than lose our standing—no matter how much make-believe is required. In so doing, we cheat others, cheat ourselves, and cheat God.

Proverbs 12:22 tells us what the Lord thinks of our actions: *The Lord detests lying lips, but he delights in those who tell the truth.* Obviously, I was not one in whom He delighted. Understatement!

I had a chance to tell the truth. Did I? Not even on my egotistical radar. I had a chance to repent. Did I? Same answer. I could not risk ruining my reputation. The stakes were too high. My smartness was hanging on the "what will people think of me?" line of egocentrism.

I can't think of one single, positive, God-honoring thing that results from that motive. What I can think of is God grieving that anyone in His creation wants to "fit in." In 2020 on *American Idol,* singer Demi Ray confessed to judge Katy Perry, "I get insecure because I don't look like the other girls." Perry's response was immediate: "There's probably not someone who looks like you because you're supposed to look like you."

God took the time to stamp a one-of-a-kind DNA into every one of our cells. St. Augustine's words need to be imprinted on our hearts: "God loves each of us as if there was only one of us." So if our uniqueness is His sweet gift to those He created, what keeps us from being satisfied? We want more, and should we get it, we will do just about anything to keep it. We will not give up our crown even when the way of the cross means we are to be glad for others who deserve the glory.

You've probably been there. Two captains are chosen. Their job is to pick the team that has the best chance of winning. Spelling bees. Dodgeball contests. Recess softball games. And if your strength does not lie in the assigned activity, you suffer the indignation of being "last (wo)man chosen." The Bible shares a story that brings that message home.[21] Judas Iscariot had hung himself after ratting out Jesus, and a new apostle needed to be chosen to take his place. There was one stipulation: the man had to be with Jesus from the time of Jesus' baptism to his Ascension. Two men met the requirements: Barsabbas and Matthias.

Perhaps I read too much into this, but since Scripture gives no indication otherwise, I have to imagine both men were pretty stoked about the assignment. I picture some heart palpitations as they wait eagerly while the apostles prayed that God would reveal the one He had selected. Lots were cast. Apostle Number Twelve will be . . . drumroll, please . . . Matthias!

I feel for Barsabbas and hope he wasn't upset. After all, he did come in second. That's pretty good, right? I mean, yes, he lost, but I hope he was spiritual enough to recognize that God did what He needed to do.

I hope.

The point is this: God's ways are not our ways. Whether we come in second or third or eightieth, that's okay. We are not gifted in all things, but we are gifted.

> God's ways are not our ways. Whether we come in second or third or eightieth, that's okay. We are not gifted in all things, but we are gifted.

For some of us, however, that does not involve facts about Kansas.

fourteen

THE PITFALLS OF LEADERSHIP

God has given you one face, and you make yourself another.
WILLIAM SHAKESPEARE

In spite of heading off to college with more confidence than when I entered either junior high or high school, there remained emotional baggage that continued to weigh on my self-worth. Having a debate scholarship alleviated some of my insecurities, and getting a job between classes in the communication department gave me the money to join a sorority, so I was meeting a lot of remarkable people who, without knowing my background, saw more in me than I saw in myself.

Some of my dearest friends came from that Alpha Gamma Delta pledge class. To this day, more than fifty years later, six of us annually travel together, adventures filled with nutty, wonderful, embarrass-our-children memories. We live for such moments.

Our first year at Pittsburg (no "h") State University (Pittsburg, Kansas), we lived in dorms that were splattered across campus. In order to hang together, we created numerous activities that weren't always endorsed by our "actives" or our house mother. Still, we persisted. I was our pledge class president, no doubt elected because I was on a college debate scholarship and had fooled my sisters into thinking I was academic and a leader—not to mention no tests about Kansas were included. Had they known more of my past, they would have realized that when it came to taking risks and being unconfident, I was the queen.

Still, being president was a step toward making myself feel important. I was the spokesperson, the representative, for a group of beautiful, fun, talented women. They had no idea the dress I wore the first day of class was a hand-me-down from my grandmother. I continued to fool a lot of people.

In the spring of our first year, Diana, our pledge class social chairman, came up with an ingenious plan. During the day, when the actives were in class, three of us freshmen girls would sneak into the sorority house and "borrow" the upperclass women's underwear. At midnight we would join a few other pledge class sisters at a campus fraternity and hang the undies on its mobile mascot, an antique firetruck.

To this day, I don't know why I thought this was a good idea. Probably because it was unsafe and immature and stupid.

At the upstart, all went according to plan thanks to a moonless, starless, molasses-black night and a group of girls who would die rather than fail to uphold the dignity of our AGD sisterhood. Despite uncontrollable giggles and dismal aim, we managed to pull off the classic Undie Caper . . . until, that is, one of the girls spotted activity through a lighted window on the fraternity's second floor.

"Run!" she gasped in a whisper we heard only because of the night's stillness.

Say no more! We ran, all right, and I, as the long-legged, fearless leader, took charge. After all, that's what I had been elected to do, right? Bolting down the unlit street, my girlfriends were in a death sprint just behind me. I would lead them to safety, and as silly as this sounds, it would validate my importance. (Obviously, it didn't take much.)

I remember little . . . except panic. For good reason. Only a couple of months before we had been sabotaged by another fraternity as we sneaked into their house to steal some cheap, "prized" trophy from their mantle. They had several and, honestly, I don't even remember why this one was special, but before realizing the danger awaiting us, we were in a virtual mud bath in their front yard. Hoses came out and the grass quickly morphed to sludge as the guys tackled us, swathing us from head to toe in muck.

Miraculously, Colleen, Pam, and I escaped into their fraternity house, and upon hearing voices, we slithered into a storage area off the half bath adjoining the kitchen. We were dripping mud, freezing, and terrified, especially when the fraternity president called for a meeting in the kitchen. These guys were ticked! For over an hour we listened to their retaliation strategies, and with each military-style maneuver, the cruelty worsened. Then the unthinkable happened.

One of them entered the bathroom to relieve himself. The wall divider was the only thing separating the three of us girls—now teetering atop the surplus packages of toilet paper—from death. How he didn't hear our knees knocking or the sludge drips plopping on the plastic wrap around the rolls is anyone's guess. Perhaps rage has a way of blinding one to the obvious.

By the time the meeting was adjourned and the frat boys left the kitchen, we were too scared to skedaddle. At first. Exiting that room was probably the gutsiest thing I had ever done—at least that week. When it was somewhat clear that the coast was clear, the three of us tiptoed out of our sanctuary, and, using the back door, escaped to the safety of our dorms, making it back just before midnight curfew.

The following morning the fraternity's house mother contacted our house mother, and we all were placed on warning. As the girls' trusted president, I could easily become the catalyst for us being kicked out of the sorority. So much for feeling important.

I guess no lesson was learned because . . . here we were a few weeks later, once again tempting death. Or, far worse, being excommunicated from our beloved Alpha Gamma Delta sorority, the one place where I believed I mattered.

Now . . . sprinting down the brick street after believing we'd been spotted, there was no containing me. I, the valiant trailblazer, would redeem myself by leading us to safety. Go me! I remember turning back to see how my sisters were faring, windmilling my arms in exaggerated circles for them to speed up. They weren't far behind, and not seeing anyone on their heels, we appeared to be safe—until, that is, I met up with an unmarked crater in the center of the road.

It wasn't just a trip and tumble. Not a simple face plant onto bricks. Oh, no. I fell into a manhole the size of Idaho.

One minute, loping along. The next? Taking a short cut to China. This potential for sister-bonding was not going down smoothly.

And neither did I.

No warning cones. No caution lights. Nothing. Just a hole in the middle of the street, a hole so big it devoured me, with both long legs, split apart, no less, entering at the same time. My knees, after cracking like splintered bats on a huge steel pipe at the bottom of the unmarked pit, were throbbing as I crawled out. I was left to anticipate a pledge class of sorority sisters holding their hearts, panicked over losing their heroic leader. Which would explain the silence.

They were all there, all right, but it wasn't their hearts they were holding. They were clutching their stomachs, lying alongside the street, writhing in silent hysterics. All of them. No one offered to help. No one was concerned. Breathless? Yes. Worried? No. It didn't matter that I had just sacrificed my life for them. It didn't matter that a group of fraternity guys could pounce on them at any time, tearing them pretty limb from pretty limb while I would be holed up in a . . . manhole. They would rather die from muted giggles than rescue me.

We all made it back to our dorms safely that night; I limped along at the rear of the pack. As it turned out, no one was following us. No one ever had been. Just a false alarm that *just* might cause me to end up with legs now jointed by grapefruit-sized knees. That's the end of my memory of this occasion, because I was in such pain that the details between hobbling home that night and later being unable to get off the toilet without help are forever gone.

Even today, on our annual reunion, I can be sure the Great Undies Caper will be revisited. My girlfriends find it as hysterical now as it was fifty years ago.

My Alpha Gamma Delta sisters, as unempathetic as they were that night, actually were instrumental in me believing I had value, even though I now realize that there were many more rungs on my ladder of self-worth that needed to be climbed. God used them all, including these women who encouraged me to take risks. They nominated me to represent them in pageants and even Saran Wrapped my waist and torched it with a blow dryer so I could shrink a couple of inches before the contests.

My caloric intake would have starved a mosquito, but at the time it seemed effortless.

Anyway, on the outside, life was great, and with the exception of astronomy, I made respectable grades. (How one is expected to chart undependable stars that keep moving is anyone's guess.) During the summer months I returned home to Fort Scott where I made a whopping fifty cents an hour working as a nurse's aide in our local hospital. I could empty bedpans with the best of them.

My sorority days blessings came through college friends Cindy and Alice in particular. They loaned me clothes and encouraged me to get involved. Alice had a car and gave me rides whenever I needed them but never asked for gas money. It was her swimsuit I wore for a bikini pageant (more later on that mortifying endeavor to be somebody), the same contest for which Cindy attached my red wiglet in my over-ratted hair. Better friends there weren't.

Being elected to positions and winning crowns and awards was thrilling, but I still never felt like I amounted to anything significant. Granted, it was definitely an improvement over those elementary/junior high days, but the damage done during my youth had colored my confidence with an indelible red X, and my attempts to erase that mark merely left smudge marks as a reminder of the value I placed on myself. Still, I made-believe well.

At least I had that going for me.

After completing my sophomore year in college, I quit.

Not because I wanted to. Because Alice, my high school and college friend, talked me into becoming a stewardess (as they were called at the time). Since I never had been on a commercial plane *and* the life appeared glamorous *and* I (then) met the weight requirements—think Q-tip—*and* I had at that point switched my major five times and still didn't know what I wanted to do when I grew up, *and* I had just broken up with my boyfriend (again), *and*, most importantly, saying you were a stewardess made you feel pretty . . . I applied.

Alice and I both passed the initial interview and were given a second interview, which was held in Denver. Which meant I actually would get to fly. A skydiving experience a few years before had landed me in a farm lady's garden instead of the target sand trap, so this opportunity hopefully would be much safer. Both Alice and I were accepted by United, but Alice quit right after "stew school" to go back to college and ultimately end up as a successful owner of boutiques on islands where she and her husband owned yachts which they rented to scuba divers.

Silly Alice.

To this day she speaks of her flight attendant experience with the same enthusiasm she would of working as a circus janitor. As for me, I stayed on, determined to make my fortune to ensure a bright, secure future in which I would be esteemed and end up in an airline commercial.

Silly me.

For six weeks my class trained in Chicago where we learned to apply false eyelashes and configure our double buns. The scale was not our friend, and should we happen to gain a pound or two, thereby taking us over the mandatory weight limit, we were suspended until we no longer were an embarrassment to the airline.

Manuals in the early years stated that flight attendants must retain a "firm, trim silhouette, free of bulges, rolls or paunches . . . for an alert, efficient image," a mandate that later was over-ruled when someone recognized that even chubby gals could be "alert." Not to mention, big lawsuit bucks were to be made. By then I was long gone from the airline.

In the '70s the life of the stewardess was considered by most to be a sort of status symbol. Like I said: "most." Unfortunately, some passengers saw nothing alluring about our job—especially the elitists in first class on the New York-Miami run who were there to help me relive my patent-leather school days.

For whatever reason, the repeated warnings from fellow stewardesses failed to get my attention.

"I've never been so humiliated in my entire life."

"I will never, ever, ever bid for that route again."

"I've never been so humiliated in my entire life."

"If I have to call in sick or call in dead, I will do whatever it takes not to deal with those obnoxious people."

"I've never been so humiliated in my entire life."

Weighing my options, I decided it was a gamble worth taking. After all, if you have paid attention to anything I have written, you

know that humiliation was my middle name. I was more than primed
for it. Also, for a newbie like me, the reserve assignment—the starting point for all of us fresh out of "stew school"—was crazy stressful.
Occasionally we were allowed to bid on a route, but typically, because
we had no seniority, we were at the airline's beck and call(s).

In spite of the advice of others and the fact that this route hadn't
been grabbed up by the more seasoned stewardesses, I signed up and
was "awarded" the New York to Miami run, rationalizing that I could
put up with anything if it dealt with only two nonstops instead of all
the puddle-hoppers I had been flying.

Remember, this was the '70s, the days when a hot meal was served
on all hour-or-longer flights. No teensy thimble-sized aluminum bag
with four pretzels like nowadays. We're talking full service. A choice
of chicken or steak. Real silverware.

And that was coach.

First class required more. Passengers were given table cloths, ap-
petizers, the hot entrée, and a choice of dessert. Let's not forget the
free drinks. Unlimited free drinks. Not a pretty picture when you're
dealing with an arrogant, obnoxious, "I'm important and will prove it,
and you're an insignificant nothing" pool of people. And that's when
they were sober. Put a few drinks in them and the sky was the limit.
Which it actually was, when you think about it.

It took little time to realize that my patience was lacking one virtue:
patience. As the first-class attendant, one of my responsibilities before
lift-off was to take the passengers' drink orders. These people had the
manners of an orangutan. No "please." No "thank you." Had they been
my children, their arrogant noggins would have been thumped. They
were the lords. I was the lowly serf. One particular couple that seemed
to get their jollies from demoralizing us peons informed me not to
bother them unless they snapped their fingers—then I was to come
"on the double." In the meantime, they needed a drink. Snap, snap.
"On the double."

To say they were rude is like saying a tsunami is an April shower.

We had two of these trips each week, a total of eight in the month. The other stewardesses onboard, much more senior than I but savvy enough not to bid the front cabin, pitied me. Occasionally I would sneak into their galley area and vent. They understood. They too had been victimized by these muckety-mucks.

Which is why they weren't there and I was.

By the end of the month, the other stewardesses and I had come up with our own spin on the "buckle your seat belt" announcement for this particular route.

"Ladies and gentlemen . . . "— said loosely, of course. "Welcome to flight XXXX, where you will be treated with the same respect with which you treat those inferior to you, which we know is every passenger on this plane, everyone who cleaned this plane, everyone who put fuel in this plane, everyone who prepared a hot meal for you and loaded this galley with gin and tonic to make you happy, your pilots, the owners of this airline, and the lowest of the low, your stewardesses.

"In case of emergency, please stop your screaming and grab your oxygen mask. Yes, you heard right. You will need to reach up, snatch your mask, and put it over your own nose and mouth. We are aware such menial labor is beneath you, and you will want us to perform said task, but we will be unavailable. We will be on our knees praying that in the next five minutes you find Jesus. Remember Him? The one who said 'the meek shall inherit the earth'?"

(Of course, at that time I didn't know Scripture, but one of the other stewardesses did, so she added that part.)

"There are six exits on this 737, so let's be clear. In case of emergency and the front exits to this plane are on fire, your first-class ticket does not give you first rights to anything: not to wing exit access; not to demands that coach passengers help you save your overhead luggage; not to another free drink before you meet your Maker. Nada. Zilch. The crew on this plane is well aware that death is a great equalizer.

"As for your seat belt, we know it's restricting and rules don't apply to you. We are cognizant of the fact you know better than the captain when to unfasten your seatbelt and that you will unclick it before we come to a complete stop at the gate. We're also aware that should we hit unexpected bumps when your seat belt is unbuckled, no one in our union is obligated to wipe your blood off the stewardess call button.

"Oh yes, one last thing: for you rude people who think you are better than us because you happen to own a Cadillac, and we had to hitchhike to get to the airport this morning"—which, in my case, was true—"let's get this straight. 'Please' and 'thank you' will get you much better service on this aircraft. Snapping your fingers might get them cut off.

"Thank you, and fly United."

That last part about the fingers? If it wasn't true, it should have been.

fifteen

AT WHAT POINT?

You Don't Need to Be Her
You don't need to act like her.
You don't need to dress like her.
You don't need to speak like her.
You don't need to think like her.
The world already has a "her."
The world needs a "You."
LAUREN FORTENBERRY, WRITER

In his novel *East of Eden*, winner of the Nobel Prize in Literature John Steinbeck wrote this: "Most children abhor difference. They want to look, talk, dress, and act exactly like all of the others. If the style of dress is an absurdity, it is pain and sorrow to a child not to wear that absurdity. If necklaces of pork chops were accepted, it would be a sad child who could not wear pork chops. And this slavishness to the group normally extends into every game, every practice, social or otherwise. It is a protective coloration children utilize for their safety."[22]

At some point, I tell the high school girls in my Bible study, you have to decide who you are. You have to denounce your perpetual thirst for acceptance. You have to stop apologizing or compromising or bluffing and welcome those qualities that make you different. You have to search your heart for whom you want to please and how you will let that play out in your life.

Will it be when you understand that no boyfriend can measure up to the unfair expectations you have of him? Will it be when you finally accept that your family's view of you does not dictate what you become? Will it be when you wake up and realize that you're not an accumulation of your mess-ups any more than you're an accumulation of your accomplishments?

I love how Bob Goff puts it in his book *Everybody Always:* "The promise of love and grace in our lives is this: Our worst day isn't bad enough, and our best day isn't good enough. We're invited because we're loved, not because we earned it."[23] When we get to the point where we recognize that all people are on their individual journey with God, and when we become enthralled with the adventure He is taking us on, no one else's journey will matter.

So why are there cheerless people who fail to appreciate their voyage? You've met them. They are stuck in their past, replaying each embarrassing memory that failed to turn out as picture-perfect as they think they deserve. Many times they are your friendly guilt-givers, waiting for you to let them down so they can play the martyred victim until you grovel your way back into their good graces. Some even allow their sins to dictate who they are, and their mental tape rewinds each morning to start them off with a recap of their past. Yet God says His mercies are new every morning. Each day we wake up, the slate is clear. God is a God of do-overs. I love that about His generosity and greatness.

As for your accomplishments, when is enough, enough? How much applause or how many trophies does it take to finally be someone? When I was a sophomore at Pittsburg State College (now University), I sat beside Debbie Barnes in French class. Debbie was crowned Miss America in 1968 and, after a year of touring, returned to Pittsburg to resume her studies in piano. I sneaked glances at her more than I did my notes, marveling at what it must have been like to perfect the Steinway rendition of "Born Free," to circle the famous stage with such poise, and to look like a life-sized Barbie in a swimsuit. With squared shoulders and calves that touched without having to misalign her knotty ankles like I did, it was no wonder she won the coveted title.

> As for your accomplishments, when is enough, enough? How much applause or how many trophies does it take to finally be someone?

And here she was, acting . . . well, normal. Had I been she, I would be strutting around campus wearing my official tiara and sash, practicing my queenly wave while offering my autograph to anyone nearby. Not Debbie. There was nothing pretentious about her. Why, she didn't even seem to notice my piercing eyes staring at her for an hour each Monday, Wednesday, and Friday. Nor did she snicker when the professor stopped me mid-sentence from parroting what he had just said by scolding me in his flawless, Parisian accent: "Your French does not sound like French. It sounds like Spanish." What a perfect opportunity to brag about how I had taken two years of Spanish in high school, so it wasn't my fault! His reaction? "You and half the class, I presume. But no one sounds like you."

Merci me! In front of Miss America?

Debbie's French was smooth, melodic, with accents where they were supposed to be, like she had been raised in the Eiffel Tower.

Anyway, after a couple of weeks, I ratcheted up the nerve to ask her about her experience as Miss America.

Her response: it was difficult, phony (at times), the schedule insane, and she was expected to smile whenever she was in public—which was all the time because, well . . . the schedule was insane. When she relinquished her crown, the gown she wore was so heavy the shoulder straps dug into her shoulders, causing her to bleed. No sympathy. Her job was to grin, wave, and be glamorous.

I listened with empathy and thought . . .

Beauty pageants have to be one of the most narcissistic ideas anyone has ever come up with.

I couldn't wait to give them a shot.

The opportunity came the following year.

When I was nineteen, my Alpha Gamma Delta sorority sisters entered me in the Miss Pitt State pageant. Two years had passed since Debbie Barnes had relinquished her crown, so it was fresh in all our minds that another queen could come from the same batch of Kansas women. And even though it was a leap to assume I might be that woman, what else were these long legs good for? I mean, it might be a goofy dream, but someone had to win. Why couldn't I be that narcissist? Since the only tiara I had ever worn was when I was a four-year-old Halloween princess, wasn't I due?

Not atypical for these events, we contestants were to compete in four events: formal, swimsuit, talent, and—if we made it to the top five—a Q&A segment. My talent was a humorous fairy tale prose called "Prinderella and the Cince." I dressed up like a crazed "Mairy Fodgother" and told my version using spoonerisms, a twist of words. The crowd loved it.

The second night of the pageant, a standing-room-only audience heard the final five names announced. When my name was called, my entire sorority, sitting together in the balcony, went nuts. I made it. The shrink wrap worked. (You are impressed . . . aren't you?) I felt as ecstatic as if I had discovered an all-you-can-eat diet. Better than that, the audience was applauding me! I had done it. I was Somebody!

Now came the easy part, for which I was ultra-prepared, the part that would assure a trophy with my name engraved: *P-a-t-t-y R-e-g-a-n*. The part where my plastered-on grin morphed into a genuine smile. I had this!

The week leading up to the pageant had been consumed with my sorority sisters asking me every conceivable question that dealt with world peace and helping the poor. Even if no correlation existed, I could create one. Fashion trends, the electoral college, school uniforms, mollusks—you name it, I could purpose a brilliant link. That's because, as a college debater, I could talk. Contrasted to holding in my stomach and faking my cheesy grin for two hours—and that made possible only by Vaselined lips—this was a cinch. Stepping to the microphone, my confidence couldn't have been higher.

"Patty, your talent was a version of a fairy tale," the emcee began. "Of what importance do you think fairy tales are to young children?"

Within a millisecond, my brain cells jumped out of my ears, leapt off the stage, and skedaddled back to my dorm. This had to be a nightmare, no different from the literal ones I had been having for the past week leading up to this event where I wore Betty Davis lipstick and my grandmother's dress for the swimsuit part. Still, even they hadn't come close to this.

Where is the world peace part? The feed-the-poor part?

Salt beads formed on my forehead, causing my updo to frizz, a waterfall to cascade down my back, and not a few zits to erupt on my forehead. *Why doesn't the floor open up? Can I sue the person who came up with such an idiotic question? Why was I born?*

"Would you please repeat the question?" I asked. Now, anyone who has ever so much as spelled "beauty pageant" recognizes this age-old, desperate plea to implore the brain to actually engage—unlike mine. The emcee might as well have asked me to describe nuclear fusion—or is it fission?—in German. No one who ever knew me would guess the day would come when I could not talk the way I could not talk.

I began making mental plans to move to Antarctica and become one with the polar bears.

"Well," I began, stalling, yet still grinning, "the great thing about fairy tales is that kids love them, and they always teach a morale that can be a foundational tool to their values . . . "

Let that sink in. Be sure and read it correctly. Did you catch it? Hint: it's not a typo. You've got it? Bravo for you. I wish I had. I didn't say *moral*. I said *morale*. With an "e." When I failed to correct myself, my entire sorority, sitting en masse in the balcony, shrank in their seats. There would be no crown for this fool and no trophy for their mantle. Even an unschooled, tongueless tribesman living in the rain forest could have answered better than I did.

I could have redeemed myself. All I had to do was admit that saying the word "morale" was fixable. It, like poor Prinderella, could be given another chance. And then I could have talked about giving others second chances—you know, by loving the unlovely so they can become lovable because most of us don't give "different" people a chance, and we all need to look beyond appearance and see the dignity and beauty with which God created us. (Even though, truth be told, that's not especially effective when you've just been circling the stage in a swimsuit. Not to mention, I didn't believe it at that time.)

Surely I could have said *something* to cover my boneheaded screwup.

But I didn't. I don't remember what I said after that. I don't even remember who won. (Karen Cassidy.) My mind was in overdrive trying to protect myself against yet another attack of inferiority. Whatever I muttered, it wasn't enough to rescue me. Screaming silently at myself, I recognized a slow death when my lack of vocabulary met one. Had I a choice between this anguish and being burned alive, I would have lit the match.

Okay, that's an exaggeration.

I'd call it a tie.

🏆   🏆   🏆

The teens in my living room and I begin discussing what it will take for them to finally matter and to understand that they are the best God chose to make. And so are you and I. The same God who aligned the planets, painted the leopards, designed our eyes to see, and came to earth as a baby decided to bless the world with you and me. We are a work of art, and until we stop showing our displeasure to Him for creating us with our inadequacies (this is not as He sees us, I promise) and choose to have a heart passionate to follow His heart, we will miss out on the blessings this world has to offer.

Much of our Bible study discussion centers around looks, which is tragic because, in reality, God puts no weight on our . . . well, weight, or any other part of our appearance. Get that? None. He wants us to be used by Him no matter how we look. He focuses only on our hearts.

Do not let your adorning be external—the braiding of hair and the putting on of gold jewelry, or the clothing you wear—but let your adorning be the hidden person of the heart with the imperishable beauty of a gentle and quiet spirit, which in God's sight is very precious (1 Peter 3:3, 4, ESV).

If your appearance has dominated your priorities, I know a story in the Old Testament that might make you think otherwise. King Saul had proven to be not all that he was cracked up to be, so it was time to look for a new king for Israel. God instructed the prophet Samuel to travel to Bethlehem where he was to offer a sacrifice and invite the elders and the members of Jesse's family to participate. From that observance, one of Jesse's sons would be chosen the new king. Proud Papa Jesse had to be beside himself as he showed up at this ritual with his seven sons. Sort of a prelude to *The Bachelor*, you might say, but with much higher stakes and no beautiful woman competing for their attention.

Seven hunks vied for the cherished position, but with such a selection, what was Samuel to do? Without inquiring of God, he made it simple and chose the best-looking, oldest, and first in line. Eliab would be anointed king. Let the confetti rain from Heaven. Then God spoke.

"Do not look on his appearance or on the height of his stature, because I have rejected him. For the Lord sees not as man sees: man looks on the outward appearance, but the Lord looks on the heart" (1 Samuel 16:7, ESV).

So there you have it. Strike one. Step aside, Eliab. Next, please. Suddenly, a new level of stress had presented itself, for how did one look at a contestant's heart? Son Number Two, Abinadab, was instructed to pass in front of Samuel. There was a hush from the brothers, who anticipated this would be the chosen one. Nope. Strike two. Samuel received no clearance from God. Another reject. Son Number Three, Shammah, stepped forward. Strike three.

We still don't have a winner, folks. So Samuel announced, "The Lord has not chosen this one either." Fortunately, four remain. Unfortunately, we're out of strikes. And even though Samuel waited as they strutted their stuff, still there was no heavenly confirmation. I can imagine—thanks to my own episodes of rejection—how disheartened the seven almost-kings must have been.

There was only one thing left. Samuel questioned the boys' father: "Are these all the sons you have?"

Jittery Jesse stuttered as he answered. My interpretation here: "Well, uh . . . there is one more, my youngest, but, uh . . . he's off in the pasture, uh . . . playing his harp, writing poetry, and, uh, tending our sheep."

"Samuel said, 'Send for him; we will not sit down until he arrives'" (v. 11).

Picture the reaction of these brothers. Playing second fiddle is never easy, but to be rejected for a harp-playing, poem-writing, sheep keeper might be the ultimate. And now they must stand and wait for baby bro, no doubt infuriating them even more as they are forced to act respectful and unaffected in front of the mighty prophet.

With the smell of the dirty wool wafting from his tunic, David was brought before Samuel and his not-so-happy brothers. Verse 11 goes on to describe the young shepherd: *"He was glowing with health and*

> Playing second fiddle is never easy, but to be rejected for a harp-playing, poem-writing, sheep keeper might be the ultimate.

had a fine appearance and handsome features." Details which, I guess, had been wasted on the sheep and overlooked by Jesse's family, but apparent nonetheless—and yet obviously not what God was focused on.

Verse 12: *Then the LORD said, "Rise and anoint him; this is the one."* Do you see something odd here? Since they had been instructed by Samuel "not to sit down," why does the Lord tell Samuel to "rise"? Did he fall on his face when he met David? We are left to guess.

Anyway, right there, in front of his father, older brothers, and community leaders, David was anointed king of Israel, and no ordinary king at that. In total, there are 140 chapters in the Bible that mention David, far more than Abraham, Moses, or Paul. A king referred to by God as "a man after my own heart." This was important stuff!

Let's pause and revisit 1 Samuel 16:7. *"For the Lord sees not as man sees: man looks on the outward appearance, but the Lord looks on the heart."*

God chose David to be king because of *his heart*.

It is the message these sweet girls in my house, watching a video on self-worth, need to welcome. There is work to be done, for their hearts, possibly like the hearts of David's brothers, have been broken by rejection. Prayers were needed so that, unlike the seven brothers, these girls would not live in a world of regret or resentment because of their own individual tales of missing out.

David stayed faithful to the sheep-tending duties his father had given him. He didn't desert his chores or his family. He continued to obey God in the small things, listening and waiting for God to tell him what to do next. Perhaps Jesse missed the memo, for he enlisted his son David, the future king, as an errand boy, running food to his three oldest brothers who were now soldiers locked in a stalemate with the Philistines and the giant Goliath, and returning home to his father to relay the status of the war.

On one such trip, the future king heard the taunts of Goliath defying one of the scaredy-cat soldiers to "take him on"; David was troubled. Let's pick up the story in 1 Samuel 17:25.

Now the Israelites had been saying, "Do you see how this man keeps coming out? He comes out to defy Israel. The king will give great wealth to the man who kills him. He will also give him his daughter in marriage and will exempt his family from taxes in Israel."

David asked the men standing near him, "What will be done for the man who kills this Philistine and removes this disgrace from Israel? Who is this uncircumcised Philistine that he should defy the armies of the living God?" They repeated to him what they had been saying and told him, "This is what will be done for the man who kills him."

When Eliab, David's oldest brother, heard him speaking with the men, he burned with anger at him and asked, "Why have you come down here? And with whom did you leave those few sheep in the wilderness? I know how conceited you are and how wicked your heart is; you came down only to watch the battle."

Are you sensing an itsy bit of jealousy here? Those would have been fighting words for my sons. I can hear it now: "And that, big bro, is why I was chosen king and you weren't." At which time there would have been an all-out brawl, like the time they were playing ping-pong and, because Jeff taunted Adam about winning, Adam shoved his older brother through the living room wall. (Their attempt at a cover-up was ingeniously pathetic. When I returned from grocery shopping, there was my front door wreath nailed about three feet from the baseboard in an effort to disguise the two butt cheek holes left there by Jeff.) Yes indeedy, the David and Goliath story would have had a much different outcome had my family been involved.

So, back to David. *"Now what have I done?" said David. "Can't I even speak?"*

Can you feel David's frustration? He's soon to go from pasture to palace, yet his brothers, themselves terrified of Goliath, refuse to appreciate his fearlessness. But there David stood, ready to take on the giant.

Saul got wind of David's bravery and attempted to talk him out of his brazen decision. But the future king of Israel would not be deterred. He explained to Saul that, as a shepherd, he had killed lions and bears that attempted to harm his sheep. This is what he said to get Saul's attention: *"This uncircumcised Philistine will be like one of them, because he has defied the armies of the living God. The Lord who rescued me from the paw of the lion and the paw of the bear will rescue me from the hand of this Philistine."*

Saul had to be pumped! Finally . . . *finally* . . . someone was willing to at least give it a shot. He dressed the young lad in his own tunic and overlaid it with a coat of armor, topping it with a helmet on his head. But now comes verse 39, when David fastened his sword over the tunic and tried walking around: *"I cannot go in these,"* he said to Saul, *"because I am not used to them." So he took them off. Then he took his staff in his hand, chose five smooth stones from the stream, put them in the pouch of his shepherd's bag and, with his sling in his hand, approached the Philistine.*

I *love* this part of Scripture. What was right for Saul was not right for David. David was not reliant on anyone's opinion other than God's. He was not there to impress those watching him. His motive was to destroy the one who defied his Lord.

Which is what he did. After he slayed Goliath and cut off his head, David returned to his sheep. His confidence was not in his circumstances or his abilities. It was in his heavenly Father—and *only* in that Father.

Oh, if we could just get there.

sixteen

SAY YES TO FEAR?
SAY NO TO JOY

Taking your makeup off and watching
yourself go from a 10 to a . . . wait, still a 10.
Anonymous

So let's revisit those high schoolers sitting in my living room, where they speak openly about their emptiness. They, like many godly women I meet at Christian conferences and retreats, realize something is wrong. Our problem—may I include you?—is that we have faked godliness for so long that we accept our cubic zirconium personality instead of becoming the diamond God desires. Most of us are so consumed with meeting the schedules of our daily grind or doubling down on our efforts to impress others that we allow little time to give more than a fleeting thought to Christ. Never has someone deserved so much and gotten so little.

Instead, our time is spent aspiring to meet the expectations, real or imaginary, others have placed on us. Yet we know, deep down, that these motivations need to be deflected. We give others great advice when they admit their self-worth has been tattered: "God sees you

Our problem—may I include you?—is that we have faked godliness for so long that we accept our cubic zirconium personality instead of becoming the diamond God desires.

as unique, as a one-of-a kind." Yet we fail to give ourselves the same advice.

In Matthew 16:13-18, Jesus attempted to find out what His disciples thought of Him. They admitted that some of the followers had thought Him to be John the Baptizer, some Elijah, some Jeremiah, or one of the other prophets. Jesus turned to Simon Peter and asked his view. Peter answered, *"You are the Christ, the Messiah, the Son of the living God."*

Jesus addressed Simon from there.

"God bless you, Simon, son of Jonah! You didn't get that answer out of books or from teachers. My Father in Heaven, God himself, let you in on this secret of who I really am. And now I'm going to tell you who you are, really are. You are Peter, a rock" (The Message).

Get it? Once Simon recognized who Jesus was, Jesus told him who he (Simon) really was. He no longer would be a mere fisherman; he would be Peter, a rock. We are no different. Once we get a heart awakening of Jesus as our Lord, we will recognize whom He wants us to be. And I guarantee, once we value who we are in Him, the opinions of others will seem worthless by comparison.

This morning I was studying Luke 10, and even though I've read Luke's gospel numerous times, today I saw something I've never noticed before. Jesus chose seventy-two followers, paired them up, and sent them out to tell others about Him. Verse 17: *The seventy-two returned with joy and said, "Lord, even the demons submit to us in your name."*

They were tickled pink with their personal success. Who wouldn't be? They had performed miracles. Demonic forces had obeyed them. With this pronouncement they probably expected a few haloed angels to high-five them. Finally, finally, they were special. The bragging rights were theirs. I can just hear that evening's campfire talk.

"Great day on the lake today, boys. My nets pulled in enough trout to break a camel's back!"

"Oh yeah? Yesterday, my kid won the blue wreath at the Sinai fair in the sheep-shearing contest!"

"Not to name-drop or anything, but you know that little mission trip I just went on? All I had to do was to use the name of Jesus, and I commanded Satan's demons to go or do whatever I told them to. My wish was their command."

I mean, seriously, who can top that? Except, and here's the shocker, Jesus isn't impressed. He listens to His followers rejoice in their conquest and then responds.

"I saw Satan fall like lightning from heaven. I have given you authority to trample on snakes and scorpions and to overcome all the power of the enemy; nothing will harm you. However, do not rejoice that the spirits submit to you, but <u>rejoice that your names are written in heaven</u>" (vv. 18-20, emphasis mine).

Poor guys just can't get it right. According to Jesus, the only thing we should celebrate is . . . not our abilities (even though the world tells us the opposite) . . . and not even what Jesus has empowered us to do (which, for far too many Christians, gives them their bragging rights). In his book *Traveling Light*, Max Lucado speaks to our need to brag: "The maker of the stars would rather die for you than live without you. And that is a fact. So, if you need to brag, brag about that."[24]

Our joy, our delight, our reason for living should come because we are on a journey that will end eternally with God. Our money, power, looks, status, intelligence, creativity, and whatever-else-floats-our-boats—even exorcising demons—all these pale in comparison to what lies ahead for us if Jesus is our Lord.

If Jesus is our Lord.

If *Jesus* is our Lord.

If Jesus is our *Lord*.

Only we and God know the answer to that.

None of us can go back and change our past. From the less-than-perfect circumstances to less-than-perfect people we have encountered, as Christians we have the opportunity to exchange beauty for ashes and turn personal stumbling blocks into mounds of opportunity. Is that easy? As easy as herding butterflies.

Learning to accept our uniqueness by recognizing how precious we are to our Creator can be a minute-by-minute battle, but if we depend on His power, it is one we can win. This is a message I will need to impart to these high school seniors sitting in my living room. They need to appreciate their rareness and yet also recognize that others have been blessed with special qualities they lack.

But I get it. I get them.

I mean, not that I would want to change places with anyone else, mind you, but gee whiz, occasionally I do appreciate—all right, *covet*—some of those "anyone else" blessings: the lips of Angelina Jolie, the smile of Julia Roberts, the intelligence of Condoleezza Rice, the voice of Celine Dion, the acting talent of Meryl Streep, the heart of Mother Teresa, to name a few. Who of us hasn't admired the distinct qualities in others that set them apart? The problem comes when we envy what they have, qualities that we don't.

To avoid that, we must retrain our brains to focus on eternal priorities and not earthly ones. The introduction to First Corinthians in my Bible can't be clearer as it reminds Christians to be careful not to blend in with the world and accept its values and lifestyles. We must live Christ-centered, blameless, loving lives that make a difference for God.

One doesn't have to look far in Scripture to find a poignant reminder of a talented young man who made the fatal choice to ignore what should have mattered most.

Before spending a little time in Genesis 25:29-34, a little history is needed.

This account deals with the divine birthright, a blessing designated originally for Abraham by God. Abraham's son, Isaac, married Rebekah, who gave birth to twins, Esau and Jacob. Since Esau was the firstborn, the birthright determined that the family name and titles would pass to him. He was the privileged one who would be the head of the clan, who would receive a double share of the inheritance, who would be given divine rights with eternal significance.

In this case, the Messiah ultimately would come through the holder of the birthright and bless the nations of the earth. This was no fifty-dollar bank CD for the firstborn. This was the mega lottery where no one knows that you won so you don't have to move to a remote island off the coast of Peru to avoid friends and family members guilting you into giving them their just due. Just sayin'.

But like many, Esau failed to appreciate the birthright's value and sacredness. Let's pick up the story in verse 29:

Once when Jacob was cooking stew, Esau came in from the field, and he was exhausted. And Esau said to Jacob, "Let me eat some of that red stew, for I am exhausted!" (Therefore, his name was called Edom.) Jacob said, "Sell me your birthright now." Esau said, "I am about to die; of what use is a birthright to me?" Jacob said, "Swear to me now." So, he swore to him and sold his birthright to Jacob. Then Jacob gave Esau bread and lentil stew, and he ate and drank and rose and went his way. Thus, Esau despised his birthright.

BIG mistake, Esau. *Bigger* than *big. Biggerest* would work, and yes, I think I will make that a word.

Theologian John Calvin explains it well. "It would have been his (Esau's) true wisdom rather to undergo a *thousand deaths* (italics mine; –PL) than to renounce his birthright; (sic) which, so far from being confined within the narrow limits of one age alone, was capable of transmitting the perpetuity of a heavenly life to his posterity also."[25]

A little confusing, I know. And yes, I had to read that paragraph four times myself to understand it, but the point is this: Esau didn't only mess up his life, he royally ruined the future for all those following in his family line. In other words, his choice was a forevermore screwup.

When Esau chose stew over salvation, his priority to fill his belly superseded his need to fill his soul. To him, having his immediate desire met was all that mattered, and conniving little bro Jacob—thrilled to share a portion of venison for the perks that complemented this hand-me-down birthright—pulled out the kitchen chair, placed the napkin around Esau's neck, and fed him like a baby.

I share this Scripture to help the girls understand how easily we can get out of God's will when we lose our focus on what matters most to Him. Esau was all about the immediate, as are these young gals who are convinced that their needs to be popular, to fit in, to be concerned with what others think, are not merely temporal fixes. Plagued with the craving to quench their insatiable thirst to be liked and fearing that others may not approve of who they are, if not corrected, will permit these mind games to determine the rest of their lives. And not in a good way.

Counselor Edward T. Welch writes that allowing others to control our self-worth causes us to fear them. In his book *When People Are Big and God Is Small: Overcoming Peer Pressure, Codependency, and the Fear of Man*, he lists three reasons this happens:

1. We fear people because they can expose and humiliate us.

2. We fear people because they can reject, ridicule, or despise us.

3. We fear people because they can attack, oppress, or threaten us.

"These three reasons have one thing in common: they see people as 'bigger' (that is, more powerful and significant) than God, and, out of the fear that creates in us, we give other people the power and right to tell us what to feel, think, and do."[26]

So there you have it. We will place our confidence somewhere, and when we lack confidence in who we were created to be, we place it in someone or something other than our grand Designer. We face the world trembling, fearful of what others think of us.

Welch continues. "The sin resident in the human heart (the fear of man) wields awesome power. The praise of others—that wisp of a breeze that lasts for a moment—can seem more glorious to us than the praise of God. Peer pressure is perhaps the most tragic form of the fear of man. . . .We are more concerned about looking stupid (fear of people) than we are about acting sinfully (fear of the Lord)."[27]

Anyone besides me cringing right now?

When we fear others' judgments, we are not thinking as God does. Bottom line? When we say "yes" to fear, we say "no" to joy. Our runaway thoughts do somersaults through the popularity goalposts, reminding us of our shortcomings, causing us to feel discouraged, and stealing our joy. Satan wins. And as long as we give others' opinions permission to matter, they will.

> **When we say "yes" to fear, we say "no" to joy.**

Who of us hasn't been guilty? We hold someone in awe and fear that person (just calling it like it is) to the point of allowing him or her to control us. It's a form of idol worship where, instead of placing our trust in God, we give others His place to control what we think of ourselves, a mistake with immense repercussions.

Revisiting Esau, we know that his descendants developed into the nation of Edom, while Jacob's—whose name later was changed to Israel—became the nation of . . . you guessed it, Israel. The conflict between the brothers continued into adulthood, and ultimately the nations that came from these two men warred nonstop with one another.

Centuries later, Edom was destroyed by a decree of God. Yes, destroyed. Slam! Bam! Thank you, ma'am! The Edomites became a symbol of the nonspiritual people of the world, people who cared little for

God and His will but instead were self-centered and not concerned about what He thought. All starting with a bowl of stew! And there's the rub, and not in a soothing, steamy kind of way. God made us just the way He wanted to. He has a purpose for our lives and knows the best thing we can do is trust in Him and His opinion and no one else's. He patiently—perhaps painfully?—waits for us to reflect that truth.

Oh, readers, now is the time.

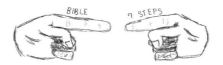

seventeen

IT'S MY PITY PARTY AND I'LL CRY IF I WANT TO

Letting go means to come to the realization that some people are a part of your history but not a part of your destiny.
STEVE MARABOLI

I wore baseball stress like shrunken Spandex.

When Dave's pitching days were over after thirteen-plus years in the major leagues, I felt immense relief. No longer would I have to try and gauge myself against other wives whose husbands were having bigger successes. No more trying to fit in with youthful, twiggy, silken-haired, perky-eyelidded, veneer-teethed, wealthy wives as we were traded from team to team.

Interesting. No matter how productive a baseball season my husband had, there was still someone doing it better, not to mention many hoping he would fail so that they could be given a chance to play in the big leagues. And who could blame them?

Coaching would be so much easier, I told myself, and in 1987, when Dave was offered a minor league pitching coach position in Syracuse, New York, I celebrated. What I didn't count on was that Satan wasn't finished with me yet. (Of course, he never is.) There still were many opportunities for my confidence to be on trial, and what better place for it to happen than in a Bible study that I, with the encouragement of Julie, the Toronto Blue Jays' Class A league manager's wife, decided to lead.

I'm going to be transparent here. Please like me in spite of what I'm about to share. Part of my motivation—actually, a huge chunk of it—for wanting to start a Bible study was I needed validation. Granted, I was passionate about sharing the Gospel with these young wives, but as usual, my self-worth was on the prideful line. It was important that I be flawless at this spiritual task. I hope you never feel the need to say the same.

Julie and I spent hours in a Christian bookstore scouring for the perfect workbook—not too elementary, not too challenging—that would teach the truth to women of various denominations. Our first meeting was in my apartment, and all but one of the players' wives attended. We started out great, but two pages into the workbook, one of the coaches' wives began to differ with its teaching. After all, there were "seven steps to get to Heaven," she explained. Accepting Jesus as our personal Lord and Savior was a nice beginning, but there were other mandates in the Bible for spending eternity with God.

Shoot me now, I remember feeling. *My patent-leather shoes experience was revisiting in the form of a pain-in-the-kazoo, Bible-know-it-all.*

Instead of encouraging these young hearts to know Jesus better, they had front-row seats to a battle of opposing opinions. No matter how hard I tried to convince this woman to "agree to disagree" on some matters, it was futile.

Mercy me, I bet Beth Moore never had to deal with such a dissident. Even as a Christian Bible study leader, I was inadequate.

After three weeks of this, I set up a private meeting with the contrary wife so we could discuss how unproductive these studies were becoming. We attempted to work out our differences, but I'm not sure anyone was any closer to the Lord at the end of that summer than they were at the beginning. Including me.

So, rather than mending my shattered confidence, baseball shredded it. Surely I could find *some* place where I could be valued. Couldn't I?

Answer: Uh . . . no.

I will call the argumentative wife Norma. Norma grew up in a church that clung to legalism like Shrink Wrap to a pickle jar. Almost weekly she would challenge what we discussed, and when I needed to return to Kansas for a week, it was she who volunteered to lead the Bible study. Julie was headed to Florida the same week, so there we were, with no excuse not to let Norma lead the group that week. Okay, there is that little thing of how I could have chosen not to be a wimp and addressed the elephant in the room, but then I risked Norma being mean to me and talking behind my back. After all, elephants really are cute, and some are harmless, so hopefully that would describe Ms. Know-It-All.

Are you seeing a problem here?

Well hold on. It gets better.

The week I returned, the wives indicated they didn't want to continue with Norma's "Seven Steps to Heaven," a legalistic doctrine taught by her church and one she shared as "truth" with the young, impressionable wives. I had to do something, so at our next Bible study I came prepared; we discussed the difference between man-made laws versus what the Bible says.

Norma opted not to attend any more get-togethers, but I learned that James 3:1 was not to be taken lightly. *Not many of you should become teachers, my fellow believers, because you know that we who teach will be judged more strictly.*

God certainly had my attention. It would be a looooong time before I would brave another Bible study. It would not, however, be the end of my rejection experience as a coach's wife.

A few years after instructing in the minor leagues, Dave was offered a major league job as the Chicago White Sox bullpen coach. As a veteran wife, I looked forward to making more than $36,000 a year, as well as meeting a new group of baseball wives.

The second part didn't happen. Most of the players' wives were childless; I had three sons and two stepdaughters. The players' major league salaries had skyrocketed by that time, and the wives, with bodies the size of Nordstrom mannequins—did I mention they had no children?—slinked onto the Comiskey Park runway with the grand entrance typically saved for *Project Runway* fashion shows. Chanel purses matched high heels; a personal hairdresser was flown in from Montreal; and one-eighth karat wedding rings had been traded in for five-to-ten karat versions. I could soooo relate to Erma Bombeck, who once wrote about fashion junkies who looked better walking their pedigree dogs than she did on her wedding day.

What I couldn't figure out was why they welcomed rookie wives whose husbands were traded there or were being promoted from the minor leagues, yet I wasn't given a chance. "You have no idea how much fun I am!" I wanted to scream.

At the games I would hear stories of their adventures in Chicago and sulkingly question why I had not been included, again reliving my Yankee metal fan experience. I justified their unfriendliness, convincing myself that coaches, given the power to release, send down to the minor leagues, or bench their spouses, were a natural enemy. Blaming my exclusion on Dave made it much more palatable. All I know is it was a loooooong six months, and I couldn't wait to get back to Kansas.

Where people were nice.

When the baseball season ended, I celebrated. The problem was, Dave had been rehired to return the following year. Something had to change.

My off-season prayer was that God would allow some of the husbands of the wife ringleaders to be traded or released so there would be a new batch of women who, hopefully, would not have hearts of molten lava and would give me a chance to be the delight I was.

Typical of God, He had other plans.

A few weeks after I arrived home, God began showing me that the ball was on my side of the infield. It was time to stop dwelling on the negative and use my talents for His glory instead of my personal self-worth.

By winter's end, I had a plan. I would start a softball team and a Bible study. After all, I had played competitive softball for several years and could use my skills to organize the wives to play for charity, and even though my minor league experience hadn't exactly become a Focus on the Family pamphlet on how to lead a Bible study, I hopefully had learned something from my ineptness.

Once that decision was made, I'm pretty sure a harp strummed from the Heavens. I ran the idea by Dave, who, in his typical flatlined fashion, answered that it "probably couldn't hurt." The worst they could say was no, which, of course, was basically the nonverbal cue I had gotten from them the previous season.

Maybe I could get used to it.

I contacted Grace, the lady who was assigned to work with the White Sox wives, and presented my ideas. She thought they were do-able and we got to work. By the time our family arrived in the Windy City, Grace had found us a ballpark meeting room for our Bible study and had scheduled softball games to benefit a home for abused women.

Terrific, I thought. *Now all I have to do is get the snooty, scrawny, narcissistic girls on board.*

Opening Day, 1990. Grace met me at Comiskey Park shortly before game time and pointed out the new wives as they entered the ballpark. I didn't need her help. They were more than recognizable. They were twelve years old, wore size minus-four designer outfits, and boasted diamond rings that no woman in her right mind would ever get weighed wearing. I, on the other hand, think I had on a blousy top to disguise the weight I still hadn't lost from childbirth . . .

. . . six years before.

I approached the returning wives first. Surprisingly, they were receptive. *Perhaps I look like a new wife to them,* I told myself. *A new wife who just happens to own the same outfit some coach's wife wore multiple times the year before. Not that they would have remembered.*

Regardless, they seemed rather excited. Well, not in the hip-hip-hooray sort of way. But they didn't tell me to go drown in Lake Michigan. This was an improvement. I was on a happily-ever-after high. Bonding time was on the baseball horizon.

Now it was time to meet the new wives. The first two were thrilled. Maybe because they wouldn't have to go through the not-so-subtle period of interrogation that every new wife endures. Fitting in. Making friends. You know, what I hadn't been able to do.

Grace then pointed to "Sharon," a stunning young gal, dressed for success, hair poofed and sealed, seated on an aisle several rows up from the others. Now emboldened because—as of yet—no one had slapped me unconscious, I confidently marched up to her seat, knelt in the aisle, smiled, and said, "Are you Sharon?"

As I squatted on the step so as not to impede anyone's view of the pregame ceremonies, she glared at me like I was on the FBI's Most Wanted list.

Seriously? This was becoming a pattern.

Perhaps my cheesy grin was too pushy.

I frowned.

She hissed as she spoke. "Do you have a problem with that?" Horns sprouted through her tightly sculpted coiffure, the venom on her blood-red lips my first suspicion this wasn't going well. Her *I'd-like-to-squeeze-your-face-until-your-eyeballs-squirt-out-of-their-sockets* glare was confirmation.

It took me a few seconds to respond to the vitriol oozing from Sharon's lips.

"Uh . . . uh . . . uh . . . no . . . I . . . I . . ."

I stammered like a broken jackhammer.

But then—*ding, ding, ding!*—I got it! She thought I was an annoying fan wanting to bug her. Yes, that had to be the problem. It was nothing personal.

"Oh, I'm sorry. I didn't introduce myself. I'm Patty LaRoche. My husband is the bullpen coach for the White Sox."

Picture Dirty Harry at high noon with finger on the trigger. "Like I said, do you have a problem?" As fast as you can say "You're an idiot," I was back in junior high, strolling across the YMCA dance floor to ask Float to dance, only to be told no in front of his acne-faced guy pals. What little dignity I had when I walked up those stairs at Comiskey Park had vanished like ships in the Bermuda Triangle. Or like me in that Idaho-sized hole in that Pittsburg, Kansas, street. Or like me wearing those stupid, ugly patent-leather shoes.

Maybe Shamer Sharon had the power to try and hurt me, but she did not have the power to decide my worth.

Which is why it makes no sense that I let her. It was painfully obvious that self-worth is capable of having a miserably short shelf life.

At that moment I knew how Jonah (from the Old Testament) felt after he had been instructed by God to witness to his evil enemy, the Ninevites. Of course, he spent three days in a whale's belly before he reluctantly obeyed, and I definitely wasn't going to give this pointless questioning anywhere close to three minutes, much less three days, but I found great comfort in the fact that Jonah's story took an incredible turn.

> It was painfully obvious that self-worth is capable of having a miserably short shelf life.

The people of Nineveh agreed to repent, to know the same God Jonah served. But this result was not on Jonah's bucket list. So ticked off is Jonah that we find him curled up under a homemade shelter, fuming that these evil people have been shown mercy. (At that moment, I could so relate.) God then created a huge plant for shade, and Jonah got happy again. Also, short-lived.

The following day God prepared a worm to eat the plant, causing Jonah to become faint from the heat. He was furious and told God so.

Look at how God responded:

"You have been concerned about this plant, though you did not tend it or make it grow. It sprang up overnight and died overnight. But Nineveh has more than 120,000 people living in spiritual darkness, not to mention all the animals. Shouldn't I feel sorry for such a great city?" (Jonah 4:10, 11)

I certainly didn't need a creepy worm to get involved. Then again, maybe that's what I was dealing with. Maybe Sharon was a creepy worm. Bible study or not, this egotistical woman was about as approachable as a cattle prod. I started my graceless exit, rising from my squat with fists clinched, and for more than a brief moment thought of leaving claw marks on this demon woman's perfectly chiseled cheekbones.

"No problem," I responded, nearing tears but refusing to show it. "I was just starting a Bible study and a softball team for the wives and thought you might be interested. Sorry I bothered you."

As I turned to leave, the creepy worm said something that made me shudder.

"I'd love to join."

Over my dead, rejected body, I told myself.

Did that make me prideful and selfish?

Probably.

"I'll give you a call," I muttered, never looking back.

🏆 🏆 🏆

Our softball team was winless that summer, but we had a blast. Grace booked us against legitimate teams who took the game much more seriously than we did. Nevertheless, we had fun and raised an ample amount of money for a battered women's shelter.

Sharon, our third baseman, was my kind of player. She dove for balls, unphased that her acrylic nails cracked as she slid across the infield, showed up for each practice, and most importantly to the fans, looked adorable in her uniform.

Then again, she'd never had children.

And, as I need to remind you again, I recently had given birth.

But I digress.

Amazingly, there's this: if Sharon's seriousness with her softball responsibility was a 10, she was a 100 when it came to our Bible study. Refusing to miss, she participated in all our discussions, volunteered to bring snacks, and seemed to settle in and find her place because of it.

Still, whenever we were together the worm issue wiggled itself into that chamber in my brain that holds tightly to the kajillion moments of rejection I ever endured. It didn't take me long to question our original encounter. I let Sharon know how insecure I was with our introduction. Her explanation shocked me.

"We came from a team where African-Americans weren't accepted. I never fit in, and I vowed then that if we ever went to another team, I wouldn't allow myself to be rejected like that." She was determined to pay back us white folks who had made her life miserable. I just happened to be the first Caucasian who approached her.

No surprises there.

Sharon had done what many of us do. Given enough rejection, we build walls of self-protection and refuse to let anyone in. We are hurt and won't give ourselves a chance to use our talents or grow our friendships. All because some other insecure people—who undoubtedly have their own stories of inadequacy—throw their poisonous darts at our fragile egos. And instead of turning away to avert the pain, we thrust out our bulls-eyed, painted chests and profess, "Bring it on."

John Steinbeck understood from where that damage was birthed. It's reflected when he lets one of his *East of Eden* characters, the

> Given enough rejection, we build walls of self-protection and refuse to let anyone in. We are hurt and won't give ourselves a chance to use our talents or grow our friendships.

Chinese butler, Lee, explain the Cain and Abel story: "I think this is the best-known story in the world because it is everybody's story. I think it is the symbol story of the human soul . . . The greatest terror a child can have is that he is not loved, and rejection is the hell he fears. I think everyone in the world to a large or small extent has felt rejection. And with rejection comes anger, and with anger some kind of crime in revenge for the rejection, and with the crime guilt—and there is the story of mankind. <u>I think that if rejection could be amputated, the human would not be what he is</u>. Maybe there would be fewer crazy people. I am sure in myself there would not be many jails. It is all there—the start, the beginning. One child, refused the love he craves, kicks the cat and hides the secret guilt; and another steals so that money will make him loved; and a third conquers the world—and always the guilt and revenge and more guilt. The human is the only guilty animal. Now wait! Therefore I think this old and terrible story is important because it is a chart of the soul—the secret, rejected, guilty soul" (emphasis mine; –PL).[28]

And so, rejection begets rejection.

It's no secret that hurting people hurt people. And, although since my Sharon incident I've never again been treated so rudely or been so publicly humiliated (at least that month), it was a turning point in the way I view people who offend me with no provocation. Now when that happens, I remember Sharon, knowing there's something deeper going on than what I see. Sometimes I'm in the mood to be patient and continue to love that person right where they are. Other times?

Other times I just pray God doesn't have to use a whale or a worm to teach me a lesson.

MAYBE LOOKS CAN KILL

Many of us don't need a facelift, we need a heart transplant.
RHONDA H. KELLEY

A middle-aged woman had a heart attack and was taken to the hospital. While on the operating table she had a near-death experience. Seeing God, she asked, "Is my time up?" God answered: "No. You have another forty-three years, two months, and eight days to live."

Upon hearing this, after recovering the woman decided to stay in the hospital and have a face lift, liposuction, and tummy tuck. She even had someone change her hair color. Since she had so much more time to live, she figured, she might as well make the most of it.

She was released from the hospital but, while crossing the street on her way home, was hit and killed by a car.

Arriving in front of God, she demanded, "I thought you said I had another forty-three years! Why didn't you pull me out of the path of that car?"

God replied: "I didn't recognize you."

Most of the teen Bible study girls' comments about changes they would like to make deal with their appearance. Lord knows, I could relate. I cringe now when I see pictures of the way I dressed when skimpy clothes were all the rage. When I retired from teaching a few years ago and my daughter-in-law Jenn hosted a surprise party for me, a former sorority sister shared with the crowd, including students, a picture of me when I was 19, standing on a stage in the middle of the football field in a bikini contest because it was, you know . . . a really pretty bikini.

Sweet Jesus, *talk about desperate!*

Michelle Graham would understand. In her book *Wanting to Be Her*, she compares herself to a prostitute. "A prostitute uses her body to gain a profit. How often I have attempted to use my appearance to gain approval from others. I have taken the body that God created out of treasure and used it as currency in exchange for love, power, esteem, and a long list of desired commodities." Several pages later, she said what all of us need to hear: " . . . in our pursuit of beauty, we somehow manage to mess things up. We have invented our own hierarchy for beauty, one that prevents us from noticing the things God considers beautiful and ultimately steals the admiration that should be lavished on the Creator instead of the created."[29]

Plastic surgery is now a $20 billion business in the United States.[30] Honestly, it's embarrassing to even write that, considering the starving people around the world. Because of cultural pressure to stay "forever young," thereby devaluing age and wisdom, people lust after the holy grail of perpetual youth. I remember the evening when my husband and I were celebrating our forty-sixth wedding anniversary and a middle-aged woman sat down at the table next to us. Sweet thing had so overfilled her lips that I expected her to quack when she ordered her appetizer. Surely she had to regret the way busybodies like me pretended not to gawk at her.

Before going much further, please know this is not a case of self-improvement bashing. There are enough experts writing exposés on topics such as "Is Plastic Surgery Sinful?" I do not profess to be in the same theological, academic operating room as they. I do, however, appreciate an article written by Hans Madueme entitled "Nip and Tuck: A Parable." Here's an excerpt from his critique concerning the "virtue ethics in the Christian tradition."

> In short, "nip and tuck" culture can serve as an old-fashioned moral parable. Cosmetic surgery is a relatively new technology, one that allows us to gratify old desires in new, more effective ways. The moral narrative here is certainly about beauty and covetousness, vanity and denial. But it is perhaps broader and deeper than that. It is about men and women, about us. You and I are frail creatures, wearied by the relentless punishments of life, dissatisfied with our lot, restless and often inconsolable, searching after something beyond us. There is an insatiable longing in our hearts, a yearning for meaning, for transcendence, for fulfillment. What are we after? What do we want? What are we willing to do to get it? Like the practiced fingers of a surgeon, these questions peel away our polished masks, revealing our true selves, our real identities. From wearing make-up to choosing friends, from buying a house to considering liposuction, life in its ordinariness, life in its spiritually charged imperfections and sufferings, reveals the kinds of people we are and are becoming. Botox culture vividly reminds us, if we are listening, that we are men and women with longings, loves, and lords. We are in fact in the full swing of a theological drama: our lives are irreducibly religious, and it is the living God of Jesus Christ with whom we have to do (cf. Acts 17:28). We will worship something—God or paltry idol. Cosmetic surgery is just the tip of the iceberg. Look deeper and you will find our vices and virtues, our hearts and our gods."[31]

In 2019, the year before Covid hit, two million people underwent cosmetic procedures including breast augmentation/lifts, liposuction, facelifts, eyelid lifts, buttock and other body lifts, leg vein treatments, Botox/fat injections, and nose and face reshaping.[32] I'm concerned that many of these surgeries are done only to make us admired or appreciated. Physical deformities are one thing, but merely filling emotional needs to attract attention or seek the approval of others can make people become their own idol. Scripture is relatively silent on this issue, but it does caution us not to be narcissistic:

> *Do nothing out of selfish ambition or vain conceit. Rather, in humility value others above yourselves, not looking to your own interests but each of you to the interests of the others* (Philippians 2:3, 4).

I love how author and pastor Rick Warren defined this principle: "Humility isn't thinking less of yourself. It's thinking of yourself less."[33]

Dr. Larry Crabb echoes that truism in his book *From God to You: 66 Love Letters.* "If you assume that Christianity means satisfaction in this life of all your desires, including the ones that lie deepest in your heart, then you live as no person was meant to live. You demand satisfaction. You live for it. You feel entitled to it. You become incapable of real love, only self-centered passion."[34]

To be clear, there is nothing wrong with appreciating beauty. God surrounded us with beauty. The problem comes when we think our personal beauty equates to self-worth. Here it is 2022 (as I write this), and yesterday, while vacationing here in Mexico, my husband relayed to me what he saw just a few feet from him. A mother was reclining on a lounge chair while her three young children played in the pool. Dave said that within a ten-minute span the woman took at least thirty selfies, each time checking her photo, readjusting her swimsuit, fluffing her hair, or repositioning her chin, all to have the perfect representation of how she wanted to look.

Is there a problem here? Oh my, yes!

God is always in our corner, wanting what is best for us. He knows that, because of The Fall in the Garden of Eden, we will sag and wrinkle, but get this: He doesn't care! His main concern is that our desires always honor Him. *Charm is deceptive, and beauty is fleeting; but a woman who fears the Lord is to be praised* (Proverbs 31:30). Given the choice, we are much better off working on the inside than the outside: *. . . that of your inner self, the unfading beauty of a gentle and quiet spirit, which is of great worth in God's sight* (1 Peter 3:4).

The older I get, the more I realize that one way to deal with my imperfections is to laugh. (You're not surprised, are you?) That's what I (and a tableful of relatives) did when my young grandson innocently described the wattle of the turkey he had just shot by pointing to my neck, citing the comparison. Not that I gave much consideration to his illustration, but did you know that the cost of a neck lift is between $4,000 and $8,000 according to 2022 statistics from "Healthcare Costs"—and that does not include anesthesia, operating room facilities, or other related expenses?[35]

Just sayin'.

🏆　🏆　🏆

These beautiful teen girls, their entire lives ahead of them, are hoping that I share some magic words, leading them into a deeper relationship with Jesus, but they would be transformed if they could just realize how God loves them exactly as they are. And that's what I tell them. Ephesians 2:10 says it more emphatically than I can: *For we are God's masterpiece. He has created us anew in Christ Jesus, so we can do the good things he planned for us long ago.* The girls don't consider themselves masterpieces, and there's a fair chance you don't either. Some of us view ourselves as a worn-out, shriveled shred of weathered tapestry, a lie of gargantuan proportions!

We are God's fine work of art. He made the choice to give us a few imperfections so we won't idolize ourselves. That nose we consider too flaring? God's design. Knobby knees? God's design. Those EEE feet? God's design. He created us and is super proud of how He made all of us unique, so why do we spend so much time wanting to be someone we aren't? Would we alter Leonardo da Vinci's *The Last Supper* by superimposing Whistler's Mother in the background? Of course not.

Only God has the right to sculpt His masterpiece. The problem is, He isn't concerned that we all look like J Lo (but good night, she is stunning, isn't she?). God wants to mold us into His image, and this has nothing to do with external looks. I pray that offers you comfort.

Philippians 1:6 (NIV) makes a life-altering promise: *Being confident of this, that he who began a good work in you will carry it on to completion until the day of Christ Jesus.*

We begin with *envy*: I want what you have. *Jealousy* starts to take root: you have what I want. *Judgmentalism* springs up: belittling you makes me feel better about who I am. Weeds in the form of *discontentment* take over: I am not satisfied with who God created me to be. Finally, *peace eludes me.* I am not enough. From *envy* to *inadequacy* in five easy steps. Medieval theologian Thomas Aquinas said this of envy: "Envy according to the aspect of its object is contrary to charity, whence the soul derives its spiritual life. . . . Charity rejoices in our neighbor's good, while envy grieves over it."[36]

People, pay attention. If we want our Christian lives to matter, if we want to mature in our faith, we have to be happy for the successes of others instead of wanting what they have. And yes, I realize it's hard. I'm old enough to remember the days when it was possible to have a party or go on a vacation or eat a scrumptious meal without the entire world knowing about it. No longer. Now we can—almost in real time—be privy to others' experiences (real or imaginary).

You just posted a selfie of you and your loved one sipping piña coladas from cantaloupe-sized stemware, your canopied beach chairs resting on white sand with tranquil aqua-blue ocean waves in the background? Even though I find some solace in knowing that many of these photos/videos fail to show the arguments that preceded them or the credit card debt that paid for them or the umpteen shots before one was perfect enough to qualify, it's hard not to be envious. . . especially if I'm at home with a blinding migraine, trying to get little Johnny's magic marker creations off the wall, doubting how I'm going to make my house payment, looking for an honest car mechanic, and trying to find time to make the three dozen cupcakes for the church raffle.

Let's be real. My reaction to your posting might not be very Christlike. Actually, I might want to dig your eyeballs out with a screwdriver.

Now, don't get all spiritually puffed up and act like you don't know what I'm talking about. It's stinkin' hard to be excited for others' cushy vacation photos when I would be happy with fifteen minutes of toilet time alone. The problem is, Scripture makes it clear we are to love, and love and envy are not friends. They aren't even acquaintances. They are—and remember this—*enemies*!

We must accept that there always will be someone who appears better off than you or me. And even if their lives are pictures of paradise, my coveting what they have as a "feel good" way of measuring up is a waste of the hours God is giving me to use my blessings to honor Him. How sad for God when I count their blessings instead of mine!

No one knows you or me better than God. He is a master in the self-improvement area. He is in the business of turning understudies into starring roles. After someone anonymously posted, "Maybe God doesn't want me to sing well, for I could end up like Whitney Houston and not Celine Dion," I started to think about ways in which God knows—much more than I—why He sculpted me the way He did. Why I must understand that everything that happens to me is under His control.

I love the story in Second Samuel in which King David was approached by a man named Shimei who pelted David with stones and cursed him, saying, *"Get out, get out, you murderer, you scoundrel,"* reminding David that his (David's) own son now controlled David's kingdom. When one of the king's soldiers asked permission to behead "this dead dog," David's answer spoke volumes.

"If he is cursing because the Lord said to him, 'Curse David,' who can ask, 'Why do you do this?' . . . *Leave him alone; let him curse, for the Lord has told him to.* . . . *It may be that the Lord will look upon*

my misery and restore to me his covenant blessing instead of his curse today" (16:7, 10, 12).

Get that? When we get all puffed up and out of joint because our feelings have been hurt or we don't feel valued, perhaps God is using that as a teachable moment, just as David said. Can we view our incidents of rejection with such an eternal perspective?

What if our attacker has a valid point, but our pride won't allow us to listen? Are there ways we could improve if we just humbled ourselves and considered what was being said? There have been times in our marriage when Dave has been critical. I drive too fast. I should exercise more. I eat too fast. My first reaction was to remind him that he isn't so perfect himself and to list my litany of complaints as payback. I was anything but humble. My goal was not to improve our relationship, it was to defend myself. Pride at its finest.

I've seen marriages and friendships and companies dissolve when warning signs went unheeded. Instead of using a little introspection, people's defenses are magnified, feelings are hurt, and no one benefits.

Let's say the comments have no basis in fact, yet we still allow them to get under our pretty little skin. When we concern ourselves with what others think of us, we are full of . . . you guessed it: pride. "I don't deserve that kind of treatment." Yet, Romans 15:1 tells us to "bear with the failings of the weak." Just like God does . . . over and over and over again. I know from personal experience.

So, shouldn't that be the attitude we have when others put us down? After all, they are showing their weakness when they purpose to make us feel less about ourselves. Shouldn't we treat them with the same compassion with which God treats us?

I think we all know the answer to that.

Perhaps had my Creator given me my way and made me look like Sofia Vergara, I would be content only with outer beauty and not seek inner beauty, and I would become vain and haughty and a plastic surgery-aholic seeking to stay that way. Perhaps God gave me the ability to find humor in almost every disastrous thing that happens in my life because He knows that if I owned mansions and airplanes and yachts I would be so overwhelmed and stressed that I would not understand the beauty of laughter. Perhaps had I been born into wealth and owned a horse and joined the rodeo circuit . . . actually, that sounds like a lot of fun and something I'd still like to do, so forget that one.

Still, I hope you get the point.

Looking to others to find our adequacy is never beneficial. We must accept that God has chosen to give others gifts we have not been given. Should we desire what they have, we are trying to do God's job for Him. God, have mercy!

Please.

> We must accept that God has chosen to give others gifts we have not been given. Should we desire what they have, we are trying to do God's job for Him.

In the past few years, a new phenomenon has emerged. Popularly referred to as FOMO, it is known as the "Fear of Missing Out." It is the opposite of FOMJ (Fear of Missing Jesus) and rears its envious head every time I think someone else is doing something cool and I'm not included. (You know, like the beach thing.)

FOMO is irrational, compulsive, and, I believe, looms near the top of Satan's tools to keep us living (er, make that "existing") in a world of discontentment. Should we indulge ourselves in this type of resentment, we will fail to recognize what God has in store for us *right now*. It's discontentment that screams, "Never be satisfied! Long for what you do not have!" Anyone fearing the emptiness that comes with not being included will cause that person to live for comfort and fulfillment. Not the way God desires we draw close to Him.

In a controlled study with ninety-one college-aged participants, researchers found that seeing social media photos of a missed social-group event triggered a two-pronged "FOMO effect": a decrease in enjoyment of one's current experience, and an increase in expected enjoyment of the missed experience.[37]

But here's the crazy part. This "envy" occurred even when the event which the participant attended was actually more enjoyable. Is that nuts or what? Here's how it could play out. If Carrie Underwood is my favorite singer and my friend surprises me with a ticket for the two of us to go to her concert, but I find out the popular girls in my class are having a sleepover and I'm missing it, I will not enjoy my experience but will long for theirs.

People, make some sense of this! I mean, we always knew that the social media addiction fed our need to stay connected, but now we are finding how equally important it is to help us not be *dis*connected. Heavens to Betsy, what if Betsy posts pictures of the BFF movie night and I'm not invited? *Any*body who is *some*body is there . . . well, except me, of course. Or what if I was invited but my killjoy parents made me go to my grandmother's 80th birthday party instead? I'm missing out—and this is never a good thing. I must stay connected! I cannot be disconnected! Or I will die!

Such is the desperation that propels people to check their texts and tweets and Instagrams the second they hear a ding on their phone. After all, there's always someone doing something in which I must be involved. Better yet, I can't afford to miss out on the news that someone has just been broken up with or failed the promotion or wrecked his or her new car. And my faux empathy is better than none, right? At least I'm involved by hearing about the tragedy. My day is better already.

The truth is, when you think about it, life is all about missing out. We cannot do it all. Right now, as I write this, I am missing out on Macy's 75 percent off sale, a tennis match with a girlfriend, and phone calls catching up on a dispute going on in my hometown. The same is true for you. If you are reading this book, you are choosing to forego some other things you could be doing. (However, good choice, in my humble opinion!)

In a new study, published in the journal *Motivation and Emotion,* researchers from Carleton and McGill Universities in Canada determined that FOMO was associated with fatigue, stress, and trouble sleeping. Whenever participants were reminded of an activity in which they were not engaging, they experienced negative emotions like boredom and loneliness.[38]

Still more studies found FOMO to also be related to greater depression, anxiety, and physical symptoms.[39]

Are you seeing the futility in this? The stress created by this complete waste of time has the potential to put us in a tailspin and prevents us from bettering ourselves. And wouldn't self-improvement be more productive? Perhaps there are steps I could take to cause others to want to invite me. Perhaps I need to diversify my life so I have something to offer. Perhaps not being part of the action is God's way of protecting me. Perhaps I need to learn contentment and pray for those who have left me out. Hard to do, I know, but I'm guessing that would be a huge God-pleaser.

If we want to be joyful, the answer is not in comparing ourselves to others, wanting what they have, or feeling bad when others have what we don't. The answer is to pursue excellence by being grateful for how God has designed us.

Dave, working as the rehab pitching coach for the Miami Marlins, along with all the other baseball personnel, received the following email from upper management. Written by Jon Gordon and forwarded to the Marlins for its athletes, I could not help but notice how the message resounded with everyone who tries to be something other than themselves.

Stop Comparing, Start Pursuing

One of the things that holds many of us back, as individuals and teams, is comparing ourselves to others. It's a trap. It causes us to focus on someone else's gifts, talents and purpose versus our own. It's what happens when we are focused on success versus excellence.

Success is often measured by comparison to others. Excellence, on the other hand, is all about being the best we can be and maximizing our gifts, talents, and abilities to perform at our highest potential.

We live in a world that loves to compare. We are all guilty of doing it. However, I believe that to be our best we must focus more on pursuing excellence. We must focus on being the best we can be and realize that our greatest competition is not someone else but ourselves.

For example, coaching legend John Wooden often wouldn't tell his players who they were playing each game. He felt that knowing the competition was irrelevant. He believed that if his team played to the best of their ability they would be happy with the outcome. In fact, John Wooden never focused on winning. He had his team focus on teamwork, mastering the fundamentals, daily improvement, and the process that excellence requires. As a result he and his teams won A LOT.

A focus on excellence was also the key for golfing legend Jack Nicklaus. His secret was to play the course not the competition. He simply focused on playing the best he could play against the course he was playing. While others were competing against Jack, he was competing against the course and himself.

The same can be said for Apple's approach with the iPod, iPhone, and iPad. When they created these products they didn't focus on the competition. Instead they focused on creating the best product they could create. As a result, rather than measuring themselves against others they have become the measuring stick.

We have a choice as individuals, organizations, and teams. We can focus on success and spend our life looking around to see how our competition is doing or we can look straight ahead towards the vision of greatness we have for ourselves and our teams. We can look at competition as the standard or as an indicator of our progress towards our own higher standards. We can chase success or we can pursue excellence and focus 100 [percent] of our energy to become our best . . . and let success find us.

Ironically, when our goal is excellence, the outcome is often even greater than success.

Stop comparing.

Start pursuing excellence today.[40]

I couldn't say it any better.

nineteen

THE WORST FAILURE?
FAILING TO TRY

Only those who dare to fail greatly can ever achieve greatly.
ROBERT F. KENNEDY

Rejection. If you have felt its sting—and who hasn't?—you're in the majority. Anyone who takes a risk, risks failure. At my 50th high school reunion dinner, classmates had a chance to share memorable moments. Some mentioned a counselor we had in high school and recalled with great clarity the words she used to discourage them from pursuing their dreams. Later, I contacted three who shared what they were told.

Barb, after taking the ACT, wrote in an email (I have left these unedited and thus in original form):

The results: I was sent a time to meet with the counselor at our high school. I can still feel "the sting" when hearing the results. I was told very clearly I would fail at a major university, make Ds at the area college, and might make Cs at the local community college. What a shock, as I was a fairly good student in high school! I knew I was very social, but never had I considered not going to college. Embarrassed by the results, I never discussed them with anyone.

50 years later: At my 50th high school reunion we were asked to share a memory. For some reason, I shared this experience. I wanted my classmates to know how over the years I held so many of them in high esteem for many reasons . . . mainly their high school and post-high school successes and experiences. It felt good sharing that night; I was among friends. I asked if anyone else had a similar experience, and to my amazement, hands popped up in that crowd of 68-year olds. It made me sad.

Side note: Barb went on to become a middle school principal after receiving her BS, MS, and EdS degrees.

Marilyn:

I am not a good standardized test taker and my ACT score was less than stellar. _____ told me I was not capable of becoming a nurse and should consider something else besides college and nursing. I was devastated to say the least and never told anyone, not even my parents. Proved her wrong and graduated from KU with a Bachelor of Science degree in Nursing, went on to get a Master's in Nutrition at Arizona State University. The Master's in Nutrition allowed me to become a Registered Dietitian and then I added a Certification in Diabetes Education to the list. I will have to say every time I did something academically, I could still hear _____ telling me I would not amount to much and I questioned myself more than I needed to. However, I am one of the lucky ones as I have a wonderful, supportive family to cheer me on.

Christi (this presented in condensed format):

When I met with _____ for our scheduled session in the spring of 1970 she asked what I wanted to do after graduation. I responded about going to college and becoming an American History teacher at the high school level. She immediately informed me I hadn't done "that well" on the ACTs, so wasn't sure college was really go-

ing to work out. When I mentioned that I made excellent grades (only B was in geometry), she said that wasn't relevant. . . . Since I did "ok" in the sciences, nursing might work.

Christi went on to become a critical care nurse. This was how she ended her email:

. . . After talking to Marilyn and hearing about others with stories about _____, it makes me wonder how many students she negatively affected. Did she talk them out of college or going into something they liked? One would have assumed that a guidance counselor was on staff to be helpful, supportive, and instrumental in assisting the students positively with their future desires. Not her! It is sad to consider how her attitude may have influenced others who had potential but didn't have the means, assistance, or confidence to strike out on their own and find their path.

When I hear these stories, like Christi, I too wonder how many other teenagers were told their dreams were out of reach, so they settled. The three classmates of mine were fortunate to come from loving, encouraging families that made them believe the risk was necessary for their success. But what about those who weren't? We all know that many times real success requires sacrifice, disappointment . . . sacrifice, disappointment . . . sacrifice, disappointment . . . and a never-quit attitude, much like the video I saw on YouTube with the poodle with his head in a bucket, running into a wall, over and over. Not a few biblical women, second-class citizens in those days, took risks.

- When the evil Sisera fled to Jael's tent, she gave him a cot, tucked him in, and drove a tent peg through his skull after he fell asleep to ensure victory for the Israelites.

- Abigail took it upon herself to meet and bestow food and drinks on David and his raiding party as they were traveling to kill her belligerent husband.

- Rahab, the prostitute, helped the Israeli spies escape.

- Ruth, a Moabite, left her family and native land to follow her mother-in-law, Naomi.

- The hemorrhaging woman, after twelve years of bleeding, reached out to touch the hem of Jesus' garment.

- Mary poured perfume on the head of Jesus in spite of the fact that Jesus' followers chastised her for honoring him so.

Change will come only when we women follow the model of persistence set by the characters listed above, take a few bumps and bruises, and refuse to give anyone else the power to make us believe we are less than God created us to be.

One Christmas a student left a card in my mailbox. On it she had written: "If you are afraid of falling, you will never fly." I know far too many Christians who have allowed others' opinions to dictate who they are, who are so afraid of falling that they refuse to use their God-given talents to attempt to soar.

- "I've always wanted to start a Bible study, but my friend tells me no one will come because I'm not an expert on the Scriptures."

- "I'd love to sing in the choir, but my husband says there are plenty of others with better voices."

- "I've dreamed of going on a mission trip, but my mother is convinced I'll be killed if I leave this country."

- "I keep thinking how cool it would be to start a tea room, but what if people don't support it?"

- "I know I should be bolder as a Christian witness in my neighborhood, but what if they talk behind my back?"

- "I have a great idea for a book, but what if I can't find a publisher or it gets horrific reviews?" (That one was from me.)

I fear too many people end up with a life of regret instead of one of adventure. Given the choice, I'm pretty sure we all know which memory most people want to describe their life. So how do I impart to those teens circled in my living room sufficient pearls of wisdom to persuade them to buy into the importance of the choices they need to make?

If these girls are going to spend their adulthood with a sense of adventure and not regret, they must stop wasting the rest of their lives trying to please others, and they must know that there will always, always be someone who will tell them they aren't good enough, and that comparing themselves to others is not God's best.

I pray you are not one who refuses to take risks and ends up having little to show for your life. I pray you are not so terrified of being adventurous that you fail to ask yourself what the worst thing is that can happen if you fall off the paddleboard or forget your PowerPoint for your presentation or sing off-key in karaoke. In *Life Is Like a Musical: How to Live, Love, and Lead Like a Star*, author Tim Federle writes:

> "... if you sit back and never get up, you'll be self-diagnosing a terminal illness known as Wondering. The symptoms of Wondering include: (sic) stressing out about who you could have been, what you could have accomplished, where you could have lived out your happiest days."[41]

I am confident you do not want to be that person. And neither do I.

In chapter five we looked at the excuses Moses used when God directed him to lead a few million Israelites out of Egypt and into the Promised Land. An eleven-day trip turned into forty years because of the stubbornness and disobedience of the Israelites.

Can anyone relate?

My hand is raised here.

With brother Aaron's help, Moses finally obeyed, and one day God told Moses to climb Mt. Sinai to chat. There He gave the prophet instructions on issues ranging from the tabernacle's design to the expected behavior of the Israelites. Instructions that took forty days and forty nights to deliver. And then, with His own holy finger, God inscribed two tablets containing The Ten Commandments and handed them to His chosen leader. Priceless!

Meanwhile, back at the campfire, the natives were restless. Brother Aaron told his band of malcontents to hand over their gold (the same gold God provided for them when they escaped Egypt) so he could make a calf-idol for them to worship. No one objected. No one!

Pretty soon they were do-se-do-ing around the golden calf, an asinine, idolatrous act not unseen by God, who alerted Moses to their shenanigans and shared His plan to take them out. Moses intervened, reminding God of His promises to Abraham, Isaac, and Israel years before to give His chosen people the Promised Land. God listened and relented.

The Israelite leader knew what to expect as he headed down the mountain. God had filled him in on what he would encounter when he reached base camp. Let's pick it up in Exodus 32:19, 20: *When Moses approached the camp and saw the calf and the dancing, his anger burned and he threw the tablets out of his hands, breaking them to pieces at the foot of the mountain. And he took the calf the people had made and burned it in the fire; then he ground it to powder, scattered it on the water, and made the Israelites drink it.*

Someone was not a happy hiker. He threw down and fractured what God had given him. Read that again. Moses destroyed what had been handed him by God because of the actions of others!

Readers, listen up. This is super applicable. When God gives you something (talent, beauty, intelligence, the ability to make a rhubarb pie, or even the Ten Commandments), do not allow others' negative

Someone was not a happy hiker. He threw down and fractured what God had given him. Moses destroyed what had been handed him by God because of the actions of others!

words or behavior to cause you to throw that blessing away. If you take nothing else from this book, please take that last sentence. And please, no more excuses.

I encourage those I meet to risk failure and do something crazy: take a painting class; learn French (unless you have a Spanish accent); perfect the Cat's Cradle; ride a mule to the bottom of the Grand Canyon; or, if you're crazy nuts, write a book. Maybe it's time we ask ourselves where we have been equipped or what dream we might have and then go for it. Sometimes these crazy ideas pay off, even if the only thing they make richer is knowing we had the guts to take a risk.

Sometimes, however, taking a chance might be a really, really stupid thing to do.

🏆 🏆 🏆

I hold to the standard that there is nothing—no testing, no circumstance—that is so hopeless that, through sheer determination, I cannot find a way with which to embarrass myself and others. It's a matter of one teensy misstep followed by a medium-sized misstep and then, drum roll please, a nuclear misstep.

"She's choking."

I heard him say it. Not clearly, mind you, because his speech impediment made him difficult to understand. But if ever my classroom bulletin board's reminder that "Body Language Screams" came true, it was now.

I had just driven up to our sons' little league fields in Hinsdale, Illinois, where they were playing on baseball teams for the summer. Dave was coaching for the Chicago White Sox and was at Comiskey

Park that evening. Jeff, Adam, and Andy piled out of the car and ran to their respective fields while I searched for a parking spot.

It was then I spotted Marvin and Vera, a special needs couple who operated our little league scoreboard. Marvin was waving frantically, trying to get someone's attention to help his wife, who had just fallen.

Trauma! I bounded from my illegally parked car and loped to the rescue. I heard Marvin's garbled words: "She's choking."

Not to worry. Remember Kathy, my girlfriend who was with me when my hair was mutilated by the bus dashboard metal fan? She had once performed the Heimlich on a choking passenger and had filled me in on the details. Surely that qualified me to save a life! All I had to do was to wrap my arms around Vera's midsection, clasp my hands, and thrust upward. Whatever was lodged in her throat would be expelled.

Cherishing a mental image of indescribable heroism, I said to myself: *I can save her.* But I ignored my other voice, which I will refer to as "Common Sense." It repeated: *You're an idiot,* a voice I would ignore if this might mean I had a chance to save a life. Of course, there weren't many areas in which I was as unqualified as this, so I was very much into proving my value.

Vera somehow had landed in a sitting position. I immediately knelt behind her and threw my arms around her midsection.

Er . . . let me rephrase that.

I *tried* to throw my arms around her midsection, and would have, except for the extra hundred-plus pounds she carried there. My hands couldn't meet to lock. Squeeze as I did, there was still about a ten-inch gap between my fingertips.

By now the baseball crowd was beginning to congregate. Squashing my cheek into the victim's spine, I began centipeding my fingers toward each other, managing to close the gap to about two inches. The difficulty was, apart from supporting Vera, now moaning and losing consciousness, within seconds she began limply collapsing to one side.

Taking me right along with her.

Simultaneously, we conked our heads on the ground. I quickly jumped up, squatted, planted my feet, and attempted to yank her back into a sitting position.

The game warmups were suspended as the emergency developed.

Sweet Jesus! From hero to humiliated in one easy step! (All this was going through my head.) *Just what I need is attention—yet again—for being a failure.*

After barking orders for someone to call the paramedics, I solicited the help of two fathers of my twelve-year-old son's teammates. Taking turns, they attempted to right Vera, but even they were unable to encircle her torso.

Desperate to save face—not to mention, my patient's life—I improvised. I flopped Vera over on her back and began pounding under her sternum, determined to dislodge whatever was clogging her airway.

Nothing. Nada. Zilcho.

My life passed before my eyes. It seemed Vera had swallowed a bowling ball! Exhausted, I finally stopped, looked at Marvin, and said, "What is she choking on?" Marvin's eyes were bulging and glazed, so I repeated my question, this time with a little more urgency (correction: hysteria!).

"Choking? *Choking?* Why, she ain't choking. She just passed out. It happens when she gets dizzy."

And speaking of dizzy, that pretty well sums up my recollection of the rest of this story. I remember the ambulance arriving, the two "assisting" fathers running for their "we'll-be-sued" lives, and the previously curious but now hostile crowd dispersing, casting a lofty sneer of contempt as they did. The paramedics wanted a report. I confessed that I had pretty well beaten the tar out of Vera, to no avail.

After the ambulance pulled away with Vera, I sat through the ballgame, avoiding side-glance eyes of disapproval while desperately searching for someone to blame other than myself. Not. Gonna. Happen. Why hadn't I questioned Marvin before jumping right in (literally) and attacking his wife? How much of my motive in saving Vera's life was to be applauded? I mean, even I had my limits on performances for which I wanted to be noticed, and killing the score-keeper at the little league field wasn't one of them.

My most pressing concern was, and I'm sure you all are with me here, how could I keep this from Dave? Was I capable of being deceptive and bribing my sons to keep their sweet little mouths shut?

I was not.

All right, I was, but stay with me here. Dave had zero chance of finding humor in this situation. Actually, he just might kill me. Then Vera and I both would be dead. Who would benefit?

When the boys and I arrived back at our apartment, we discussed how "unnecessary" it was to share this minor little detail with Daddy, how he didn't need to be bothered with this news because he had so much other stuff on his mind. Then I phoned the Hinsdale Hospital and asked for the emergency room. I didn't know Vera's last name, only that she was the "bag lady" of that suburb. Once I was connected to a nurse, I asked for an update. She gave no details.

All I heard was this: "She's gone."

A boa constrictor was squeezing *my* airway.

Several seconds lapsed.

"Gone? Oh, dear God, *Gone?*"

Yes indeedy. I had killed Vera. Tomorrow's headline would read: "White Sox Coach's Wife Arrested for Death of Sweet, Defenseless Bag Lady." Had I just left well enough alone, Vera never would have died. But oh no, not me. I just couldn't forego my chance to play Paramedic Patty. I was fighting back tears, trying to choke out some question to find out how Marvin was doing, when Dave opened the door. Andy, our youngest, greeted him.

"Mama killed the bag lady tonight."

Dave could tell by the threatening "You will pay for this" glare I gave our youngest—and the way he hightailed it to his room—that our son was telling the truth.

Dave collapsed, clearly confused, into the nearest chair.

Dave could tell by the threatening "You will pay for this" glare I gave our youngest—and the way he hightailed it to his room—that our son was telling the truth.

Composing myself long enough to ask the nurse one more question, I began to cry. "Could you tell me what mortuary they took her to?"

"Well, why would we do that?" she answered irritably. "I told you she's gone. She's gone home."

May I confess something here? I had been sad that Vera was dead, but up until I found out she survived my torture, I honestly was more concerned with what my penitentiary experience would be like. Pitiful, I know.

I have no words to describe the relief I felt—until, that is, I realized that Dave wasn't smiling. That's because Jeff and Adam, our big-mouthed sons, were sharing their overly dramatic, distorted version of the episode. Dave sat silently for several minutes after their exaggerated babblings. When he finally spoke, all he could think about was how we were probably looking at a lawsuit.

Whatever! Some people just think of themselves, I told myself.

Two days later I returned to the ballpark. What a shock when I saw Vera walking toward me chomping on a bag of Doritos! I pounced from my car and grabbed her hand. "Vera," I said, "I'm so glad you're okay. How are you doing?"

She thought for a minute and then answered, "I'm all right, I guess." And then, clutching her sternum, she continued, "But it hurts something awful right here."

I explained that I was to blame. I apologized profusely, but Vera didn't seem to understand what I had put her through. (Thank you, Jesus.)

I saw Vera several times after that, and she never brought it up again.

My sons and Dave, however? It's a story they just kept exaggerating. Some people will do anything for attention.

twenty

THE SHAME OF SHAME

Shame is a focus on self, guilt is a focus on behavior. . . . Guilt: I'm
sorry. I made a mistake. Shame: I'm sorry. I am a mistake.
BRENÉ BROWN, UNIVERSITY OF HOUSTON PROFESSOR,
TEDX HOUSTON TALK, 2010

If there is a person alive who has been shielded from rejection's cutting arrows, I've never met him or her. I would guess that most of you can relate, and if you tell me that you can't, we'll probably never become BFFs. My gal pals and I can remember in great detail the looks, words, and gestures targeted to destroy our self-worth, and while some of us might discipline our thoughts to ignore the enemy-archer's barbs, the rest of us have allowed them to perforate our very fragile egos. If we don't take measures to denounce these thoughts, the end result can be shame.

There might not be a more joyless way to live.

So what are some of those thoughts? In John Eldredge's book *Waking the Dead* he describes thoughts that are not from God: " . . . any word or suggestion that brings discouragement, condemnation, accusation—that is not from God. Neither is confusion, nor any counsel that would lead you to disobey what you do know."[42] By accepting negative opinions of ourselves, we run the risk of adversely harming what our Heavenly Father wants us to be.

Eleanor Roosevelt addressed our personal responsibility in accepting harmful comments: "Nobody can make you feel inferior without your consent." While true, I believe her pithy answer oversimplifies the solution to feeling unworthy, mainly because there is a tension that exists between *wanting* that dogma to be true and *living* by that dogma. Roosevelt personally understood what it was like to feel shame.

"I *craved* attention all through my childhood, because I was made to feel so conscious of the fact that nothing about me would ever attract attention or bring me admiration. I was told that I would never have the beau that the rest of the girls in the family had had because I was the ugly duckling . . .

"I was ashamed because I had to wear made-over dresses from clothes that my aunts had worn . . . ashamed because I couldn't dance and skate perfectly as others did . . . ashamed because I was different from other girls . . . ashamed because I was a wallflower. I still remember how thankful I was because a certain boy once asked me for a dance at one of those Christmas parties. His name was Franklin D. Roosevelt.

"For over twenty years I was devastated by self-consciousness and fear. My mother, grandmother, and aunts had been famous beauties in New York society, and I was ashamed to be the first girl in our family who was not a belle. My mother would sometimes say to visitors, 'Eleanor is such a funny child; so old-fashioned that we call her Granny.' The big thing that eventually gave me courage was helping people who were worse off than myself."

Eleanor writes that in 1910 her husband, a New York state senator, held several meetings in their home with eighteen other assemblymen who were warring against the political injustices of Tammany Hall. Eleanor visited with the men's wives only to find that they were spending their days and nights in "lonely hotel rooms.

"I found that by trying to cheer them up and by trying to give them courage, I developed my own courage and self-confidence. Fear is the most devastating emotion on earth. I fought it and conquered it by helping people who were worse off than I was. I believe that anyone can conquer fear by doing the things he fears to do provided he keeps doing them until he gets a record of successful experiences behind him."[43]

That sounds pretty inspirational, doesn't it? Except, that is, for a few of those words in the last sentence: " . . . until he gets a record of successful experiences behind him." What happens if that never happens? Or happens only occasionally?

I have failed at more things than I can count. (Trust me, what you have read up to this point is just the tip of my embarrassment iceberg.) Most of the time, in hindsight, I find these episodes funny, recognizing that no one likes to be around thin-skinned people who don't take laughter seriously.

> My successes or failures do nothing to alter who I am in Christ. I purpose to be identified with him and him alone, not a "record of successful experiences."

Other times I'm just embarrassed by the messes I get into. Whatever my response, there is one constant: my successes or failures do nothing to alter who I am in Christ. I purpose to be identified with him and him alone, not a "record of successful experiences."

In 2 Corinthians 5:17, Paul brought exciting news: *Therefore if anyone is in Christ, he is a new creature; the old things passed away; behold, new things have come.* Does that energize you like it does me? Put another way, if we have made Jesus the Lord of our lives, we are changed. We are the new, improved model.

Still not convinced?

Well, it's true. From caterpillar to butterfly, we can't go back. And because of that, our God-confidence (not self-confidence) should be through the roof. It has nothing to do with what we have done and everything to do with what Christ is doing through us. But it doesn't stop there. As "new creatures," our joy, our peace, our servant-hearts will be magnets for others who want what we have. Talk about filling a need! And here's the coolest group of news of all: God's way is eternal, not temporal; God's way is foolproof, not conditional; God's way is from the inside-out and not the outside-in; God's way is faith-based, not performance-based.

So let's back up a smidge to where there should be little disagreement. Everybody wants to be liked, right? (Okay, there probably are a handful of people with psychological issues who claim they prefer to be disliked, but I don't care to research them, mainly because I think that's weird.) The majority of us desire to have nice things said about us. To achieve that, too many of us mistakenly fail to stay true to Truth (God loves me passionately; He made a way for me to be a changed person; He alone deserves my allegiance). Instead, we seek the admiration of others.

Eleanor Roosevelt never gave God credit for her renewed self-confidence. Instead, she claimed that she found her value when she took the focus off herself and began blessing other people. We all can learn by her example, yes, but how much more authentic would our journey be if we did both: if we have faith in who we are in Christ and performed good works as a result?

Roosevelt's story is one of hundreds of thousands (millions?) in which emotional scars followed individuals from childhood to adulthood. I hope Roosevelt did overcome her shame, the disgrace that I imagine lurked below the surface, the memories that crawled into bed with her when her charitable work was done. I hope she lived by her quote and had what it took to deny consent to anyone demeaning her because, let's face it, far too many people don't. Instead, they dismiss their value and justify their worthlessness. They live in a world of shame which, when unleashed, has the potential to lead to self-destruction, not self-awareness.

I have met far too many.

- When my student wrote her eulogy speech (see Chapter 8) about being raped and another student wrote about being fondled, I understood better why they sat in the back row and rarely volunteered in class discussions.

- When my friends speak of their feelings of rejection as their husbands choose a new, much younger, mate, I understand their desire not to attend wedding showers or sermons on "Keeping Your Marriage Alive."

- When relatives turn to drugs or alcohol as a source of emotional comfort, I understand their desire to mask the guilt associated with their parents' divorce.

- When my long-time friend's husband was incarcerated for scamming his friends, I understood why her shame convinced her to avoid our school reunion.

- When I meet women who existed quietly with years of sexual, emotional, or ritualistic abuse, I understand why they (a) ignore the health of their bodies and over-eat for emotional support, or (b) glorify their bodies with multiple surgeries and diets in an effort to remain youthful.

- When I encounter individuals with life-altering medical conditions that have caused people to stare at them or ignore them completely, I understand why they hang their head in embarrassment and fail to take the risks for which they were once applauded.

- When the childhood journeys of various men and women involved poverty or homeliness or unpopularity, I understand why they adapt themselves to whatever chameleon approach will award them the praises of their peers.

Shame makes sure that if our validation comes only by our performance, we are prone to either strive for perfection or, worse, we will tolerate abuse, justifying that we are just getting what we deserve.

In the early '80s (pre-cell phone days), I was driving over the mountain pass from Reno, Nevada, to Incline Village, where we lived. As I passed a car parked on the shoulder, I noticed the driver banging the head of his female passenger into the dash. He had her by her hair and stopped only when I screeched my brakes and pulled over in front of them. (Save the comments about how reckless I was. I heard them all from Dave.)

Calmly (thank you, theater training), I walked to the driver's open window and said, "I see there is a problem here. Is there anything I can do to help?" The husband (as it turned out) tried to defend himself, pointing to a scratch on his cheek. Meanwhile, his wife was sobbing and holding her bloodied face in her hands. I managed to convince them both that they needed some time apart and helped the woman to my car.

For three hours we drove around, she refusing medical treatment, but all the while listening as I told her how precious she is to God, how He created her with some great purpose, and how she deserved something so much better than the treatment she was receiving. I addressed the benefits for her husband if she distanced herself from him, and told her that there were counselors equipped to turn their marriage around.

She shared that these beatings were becoming a common practice, but in the end, she "probably deserved them," and just wanted to go home. The police, she continued, had been called numerous times, but she refused to press charges. Hubby always promised to be better and, for a while, he was. "Until he decides to bang your head into the dashboard," I added.

Nothing I said made a difference. She was going home, one way or the other. I was sick to my stomach. What made her think so little of herself? As I write this in 2022, statistics say that one in four women will experience this type of abuse, and research shows that most of those caught in this web of lies ("I'll do better; I promise") were sexually assaulted as children. I wrote my phone number on a napkin and told her to call me, day or night. I never heard from her again.

After sobbing all the way home, I called the police. They knew the address well, but, according to them, because the victim never pressed charges, their hands were tied. This woman had no idea how much God loved her. I couldn't help but wonder what happened in her life to destroy her self-worth that she was willing to settle for so little. Possibly her own death.

Of course, not all people-pleasers are willing to go to such tragic lengths to be accepted. Most merely place their self-worth into the mouths of those who pay them compliments. Receiving enough favorable comments temporarily serves as a confidence builder. Until, that is, something happens that makes those individuals question their value, all the while forgetting that rejection is part of life—and the simple reality that no one escapes it.

One of my favorite books is *Letters to the Church*, written by author/preacher/teacher Francis Chan. His admission surprised me: "All my life, I have battled a desire to be respected by others. Because of this, there have been many times I cowered out of a fear of rejection. I took my eyes off of the future and did what was easiest in the moment. I deeply regret these moments."[44]

In Philip Yancey's book *What's So Amazing About Grace?* he reveals how he, an author whose books have sold more than fifteen million copies in English and been translated into forty languages, understands the fear of rejection. "I know how I respond to rejection letters from magazine editors and to critical letters from readers. I know how high my spirits soar when a larger than expected royalty check arrives, and how low they sink when the check is small. I know that my self-image at the end of the day depends largely on what kind of messages I have received from other people. Am I liked? Am I loved? I await the answers from my friends, my neighbors, my family—like a starving man, I await the answers."[45]

(I am soooooo with you, Brother!)

There is no one who was rejected more but deserved it less than Jesus. On the cross he endured rejection by his Father to pay for us whining about being rejected by others. So why should we think we deserve anything more?

Jesus' three years of public ministry were constant attempts by religious leaders to discredit his abilities. Read the New Testament. The leaders of his time, the Pharisees and Sadducees, spent many ministerial hours determining to destroy Jesus' reputation, particularly when he "lowered" himself to hang with sinners.

Jesus made it clear that we have misplaced priorities when we seek earthly reasons to be recognized. In Luke 6:20-22, Jesus described the people who will be blessed, and they certainly aren't the ones the world describes:

Verse 20: those who are poor

Verse 21: those who are hungry or sad

Verse 22: those who are hated, excluded, insulted, and rejected for Christ's name

Why these folks? Because they are the ones who will become dependent upon Jesus and no one else. Jump to verse 26. *"Woe to you when everyone speaks well of you . . . "*

Read that again. In Scripture, "woe" is a biggee, a red flag in the NASCAR lap of spiritual races. In the New King James Bible, woe is found 71 times in 69 verses in the Old Testament. The New Testament uses the word 40 times in 33 verses, with 32 of those coming from the lips of Jesus! The woe word typically expresses grief, but when Jesus uses it, look out! It is the grief of all grief; it is calling your child by including his or her middle name . . . times infinity. It is judgment!

Do you get it? As long as our crippling insecurities cause us to seek the admiration or accolades of others, woe to us! Jesus wants more. He knows those roller coaster attempts to be validated pit sinner against sinner. And yes, we are part of that label. We are messy, imperfect, insecure, rough-edged creatures.

If we invite Jesus to be our Lord, he wants our desires to be aligned with his infinite love for us, not with the fleeting, self-serving admiration from others. Caring too much about other's opinions imprisons us, causing us to live in a world of second-guessing everything we do and everything we are. Ultimately, we end up disappointing the one we secretly want to please the most—ourselves.

> Caring too much about other's opinions imprisons us, causing us to live in a world of second-guessing everything we do and everything we are. Ultimately, we end up disappointing the one we secretly want to please the most—ourselves.

We are reminded of the redemptive news in all of this by Michele Cushatt in her book *I Am: A 60-Day Journey to Knowing Who You Are Because of Who He Is*: "A day is coming, promises the book of Revelation, when our knight on a white horse will ride in to exact both judgment and mercy upon this earth. When that day comes, He will bestow on you and me a new name, His name. All the other names and labels we've lugged around for a lifetime will be swallowed up by a bigger and better one."[46]

Maybe you have a few names that need swallowed up. If so, I pray you have met the One who can make that happen.

twenty-one

KINDERGARTEN CHAOS

The pain that every struggle brings,
is the beginning stage of your future strength.
ANONYMOUS

The movie *Kindergarten Cop* was a lie, a masterful attempt intended to fool simpletons like me into thinking it's possible to magically transform a group of little nasties as cleverly as Arnold did. Perhaps if I were 6-foot-5, weighed 230 pounds, had 2 percent body fat and massive muscles, and spoke with a Austrian accent, things would have turned out differently. The point is, I never, ever, ever will teach kindergarteners again. N.E.V.E.R. I mean, how is it possible that children who come up to my thighs could make me feel so small?

A Christian school in Texas (not named here because I still fear repercussions) needed someone to fill in for the kindergarten teacher, so they called me. My degree, for multiple reasons, is with high schoolers, but I thought this a challenge worth attempting. Surely I couldn't screw up these innocent little kiddies in one day.

I laugh.

Entering the classroom, I was frustrated to find no lesson plans. I would have to wing it.

As the eager beavers entered the classroom, they seemed excited to have a substitute, and as I did at every opportunity in which my adequacy was at stake, I told myself this was going to be effortless. Because I was an accomplished substitute teacher. This was no biggee.

Whatever!

The kiddies found their designated spots on the floor. From behind the podium, I asked what I was supposed to do first.

"Take the milk count!" they responded.

"Okay. Who wants milk?"

"No!" they shouted in unison. "You have to ask for white or chocolate."

Once that was settled, I questioned what came next.

"You choose someone to take the milk list to the office."

"Great," I answered, pointing to a little girl in the front row. "Please take this to the office."

Had they blow darts, I would have been nailed to the cork board behind me. "She got to take it yesterday!!" they yelled, now at a much higher decibel level.

How could this be? Five-year-old feral children were inciting a mutiny.

Three choices later, all for naught, I asked who hadn't ever taken the milk roll to the office. Unanimously, the little imps pointed to Ryan, who seemed pleased to be nominated. I handed him the list and told him to hurry back, and if thirty minutes later is hurrying back, Ryan won the prize. As it turned out, Ryan also made multiple trips to the restroom, visited the cafeteria ladies, and went outside for a pick-the-dandelions-stroll. When he was brought back to his classroom by an aide and I scolded him, he said that that was an unkind thing to do in front of his classmates. They all nodded in agreement. I looked at the clock. Forty minutes down. Three-hundred and eighty-five to go.

"Now what do we do?" I asked, ducking behind the podium.

Bossy Betsie had the answer. "Now we get into our reading groups."

"Okay. Get into your reading groups."

Betsie gaped at me like I was a blood-sucking vampire. "You don't just tell us to 'Get into our groups.' You call them out by animals!"

"Thank you, Betsie," I said, trying to figure how to pinch her lips off her face with no one noticing. "Let's have the dogs in this corner."

At this point, they went berserk, like I had pepper-sprayed them or something, but truthfully, had I that weapon in my substitute teacher's bag of tricks, there would have been a bunch of burned kiddie faces that day.

"There isn't a dog group!" they howled.

"Well," I countered, not a little irritated, "there is no way I would have known that, now is there? What groups *do* we have?"

Bossy Betsie, whom I was finding more and more morally objectionable as time went on, and I would not become friends. "We have wolverines and zebras and hyenas and gophers," she announced.

"Perfect," I hissed, directing each mammal to a different corner of their cage . . . er, room. "Find your group and begin reading." Which, of course, they couldn't do because they were in kindergarten.

By the time they pulled out their rugs for a nap, I was scouring the teacher's desk drawers for a sedative.

> "Perfect," I hissed, directing each mammal to a different corner of their cage . . . er, room. "Find your group and begin reading." Which, of course, they couldn't do because they were in kindergarten.

I remember little about the rest of the day, except when the final bell rang. I celebrated, and not silently. I cheered . . . out loud. After all, it was time to dismiss the miniature monsters who had been raised by Tasmanian devils. What I didn't count on was the principal, a mother, and the mother's son, little Jacob, returning to the kindergarten classroom.

"Could you please explain to Jacob's mother how her son lost his tooth in your class this afternoon?" the principal asked with no small element of accusation in her voice.

Sheesh! I didn't even know the little rapscallion's name, much less how many teeth he had or was missing. In my opinion, Jacob's mother should have been happy his eyes weren't blood red from being pepper-sprayed.

No one was happy when I had no explanation for the question.

As I left the school building that day, I walked by the office and alerted the secretary: "Just want you to know I will never . . . ever . . . *ever* sub for the little tornadoes of terror again. Have a great evening, and God bless."

No one was desperate enough to consider me for a repeat performance. They did, however, ask me to take over a fourth-grade class for a six-week stint. Feeling rejected by kindergarteners was one thing. Thinking I could redeem myself with these upper-class kids only reinforced my belief that there will be a special place in Heaven for substitute teachers.

And if there isn't, there should be.

My assignment was to teach creative writing to nine-year-olds. From day one they tested me, resulting in a "Come to Jesus" meeting at which time I asked them what they considered appropriate discipline for students who talked without raising their hands, complained about whatever they were asked to do, and were basically immature beasts who gave credibility to defenders of capital punishment.

After brainstorming for about ten minutes, someone suggested that they should write an essay of four thousand words explaining how they would never disobey again. *Not a bad idea, I thought. Plus, it might keep them preoccupied and out of my hair, at least temporarily. And, as a side note, but not a major concern, it actually might enhance their writing skills.* I reduced it to one hundred words. It was the first time they were nice to me.

It took no time for Sophie to test the rules. She seemed nonplussed about her punishment and spent her recess with her head down, filling in her paper. Later that day she handed in her apology. For the first twenty words, she was repentant. Here are those words as written: "I talked when I was not sposed two. I am sorry. I will not do that agin. I am really, really, really . . . "—and what followed were 80 more *reallys*—"sorry."

So much for enhancing writing skills.

One day I came up with a brilliant plan. I think I even gave the Holy Spirit credit for it. We would venture outside on a little excursion into the woods behind the school to find some item God had created and bring it back to the classroom where each student would write about his or her findings. The little demons . . . er, kids, were excited. I was desperate. Perhaps they could burn off some energy and appreciate my attempt to be innovative. Or, better yet, they could disappear. There was only one rule: no live animals. Which led to a second rule: no dead ones, either.

The fourth-graders scattered through the trees, screaming with delight when they found the perfect object for their compositions. On this day I managed not to have a strong dislike for them. I actually loved seeing their enjoyment and praised them for their unique treasures. There were special rocks, arrowheads, feathers, berries, the sole of a moccasin, moss, flowers, and a couple of sticks. Thank God: no bodies, dead or alive. The kids were eager to write about their findings.

Upon entering the classroom, Joshua decided to anoint his classmates' cheeks with his prized stick before taking his seat. He recognized this was a spiritual experience since the assignment was to describe why they thought God created their object. I used that as a reminder of our objective.

Within a minute, Katie raised her hand (an improvement!) to tell me that her face itched "something awful." When I looked, her cheek was the size of a hacky sack, a crimson hacky sack. One by one the students started moaning and scratching and crying. Their cheeks, now blotchy red, were bloating by the millisecond. The principal was alerted, as was the school nurse. Come to find out, Saint Joshua's stick was sumac . . . you guessed it, of the poison sumac family.

Parents were called to give permission for Benadryl to be administered. Ice packs came from the cafeteria, and moms and dads came to pick up their children for an early dismissal.

A public stoning would have been less traumatizing.

Kindergarten was not my thing. Neither was fourth grade. Since the school went only to eighth grade, chances were slim I would be invited back.

I take that back. Chances were nonexistent I would be invited back. As desperate as they were for substitute teachers, clearly my name was permanently etched into their rejection list. Fine by me.

The local public school, apparently, was a little more desperate.

All I had to do was stand on a conductor's box and get the hundred-plus, middle school orchestra students started on their Christmas songs. I began: "A 1-and-a-2-and-a . . . " The students began. Their "We Wish You a Merry Christmas" was a cross between "Old MacDonald Had a Farm" and "Red Solo Cup." After a few frustrating attempts, including the use of a metronome with varying speeds, I dejectedly instructed the musical wannabes to break into study groups and call it an hour. It was curtains for my conductorial debut.

As I slinked off my platform, the young teens began laughing, rose from their chairs, and began trading instruments. And then a strange thing happened. They sat down and began playing—on their own—and they were incredible. All this time they had been playing the wrong instruments—those belonging to a student in another chair or section—thus pulling a big one on the ol' naïve substitute teacher.

Confirming my position as a capital punishment supporter.

Once they were where they belonged, they were an absolute delight. They did the right thing at the right time with the right instrument. Their orchestra teacher had taught them well. As I waved my wand and faked being in charge, it all seemed effortless. They realized it was critical they do their part so that each distinct sound meshed with the others.

God, our eternal conductor, does likewise. He recognizes our individual qualities and, like an orchestra, we all have different strengths. (For example, some of us are elementary school teachers, and some of us would rather have a root canal with no sedative.) Together, however, we have the potential to make perfect harmony. First Corinthians 12:27 makes that clear: *Now you are the body of Christ, and each one of you is a part of it.*

Back up a few verses and it becomes obvious how valued we all are, no matter what position we hold. If the foot should say, *"Because I am not a hand, I do not belong to the body," it would not for that reason cease to be part of the body . . . If the whole body were an ear, where would the sense of smell be? But in fact God has arranged the parts in the body, every one of them, just as he wanted them to be. If they were all one part, where would the body be? As it is, there are many parts, but one body* (vv. 15-20).

Just like an orchestra.

And somewhere near this subject, how irritating is it when churches delegate positions for which its members are not equipped, and how more irritating is it when Christians, wanting to please, accept the roles given? People are given duties for which they are not prepared. You lack compassion? Swell, you're assigned hospital visitation duty. You don't like children? (You probably started off as a substitute teacher, by the way.) Perfect. You will head the nursery. Your expertise is accounting? Well, put on that apron and chop onions for the funeral dinner.

Learn to say no, dear friend.

In Michelle Graham's book *Wanting to Be Her,* she speaks to this issue: "The body God chose for each of us—our eyes, our hair, our chest, our calves—is actually not ours. It is a tool for the kingdom. They are important parts of life, but my heart is not tied to them. Being content is saying to God, 'This is what you have for me, and I will be OK with that because I know you will ultimately use it to teach me and work toward your purpose in the world.'"[47]

Dear readers, we are not gifted the same. The time has come to start playing our position and be grateful for it. If you are the utility infielder, stop thinking you are the starting pitcher, which is sort of what God is saying in First Corinthians 12! Because, guess what? That starting pitcher probably won't be a decent pinch hitter when the game is on the line, but you, in that role, may be.

Reread these few words from First Corinthians 12:12. *There are many parts, but only one body.* How much better off would our churches be if we all understood the role of our eternal Conductor and played the spiritual instrument for which we were equipped?

And how much better off these Bible study girls would be if they stop comparing their abilities or brainpower or looks to the person seated near them. How much better off all of us would be if we refused to judge ourselves by the abilities God has given someone else.

How much better off?

I have no idea exactly how much. But I know it's a lot.

twenty-two

GOIN' DOWN

The reason why we struggle with insecurity is that we compare
our behind-the-scenes with everyone else's highlight reel.
PASTOR STEVE FURTICK

Perfect.

That's how God sees me.

Even though He knows my heart.

Which is crazy when you think about it because there's not one perfect thing about me. Oh, there are moments when I do something fairly well and feel a little puffed up, but invariably someone or something comes along to pop a hole in my egotistical balloon and bring me crashing back to earth. Take the time Dave was a pitching coach in Manchester, New Hampshire, and we were at the workout facility we had joined.

On that day I was swimming laps, completely engrossed in my typical mental pass-the-monotonous-time game of playing heroine. (Not surprisingly, none of my fantasies involve the Heimlich maneuver.) For a few minutes I am rescuing dozens of near-drowning victims whose boat has capsized, working feverishly to fend off circling great white sharks while single-handedly hoisting choking survivors into the life raft . . . and then, as if a remote control flips to the next channel, thousands of adoring fans cheer me on in my quest for an Olympic gold. No matter what the scene, I always give myself the starring role. No walk-ons for this drama queen.

But this time, just as I was gaining ground . . . er, water, someone whizzed right past me in the adjacent lane. Unfortunately, my new nature, the one that admires others' grace and athleticism and aquatic excellence, recognizing how God equips all of us uniquely, did not don the swimsuit and goggles that day. My old nature did. In case you've never met her, she's the one who is petty and immature and embarrassingly competitive.

Leisure lap time was over for this contender. My competitor was *goin' DOWN!*

Digging deeper, I demanded more of my arms with each stroke, but instead of propelling me forward, my triceps were dragging through the waves like rubbery prosthetic wings. No matter how hard I pressed, I fell farther and farther behind. I consoled myself with the fact that this obnoxious showoff couldn't be more than fifteen or sixteen years old and I was . . . well . . .

. . . not.

A few laps later, as I leaned against the pool's edge conjuring up ways to perform CPR on myself without anyone noticing, my challenger did one of those in-your-face, underwater flippy somersaults. The last time I had attempted that acrobatic maneuver—about her age, come to think of it—I ingested half the pool and almost broke my ankle, which thrashed against the concrete edge, causing a kiwi-size knot to appear.

You can imagine my devastation when my opponent and I completed our workout (my twenty laps to her more than forty) to see that she was no spring fish after all. We matched wrinkle for wrinkle! I had to know her secret. I decided to ask.

Silly, silly me.

As luck would have it, she actually had seen a few things I was doing wrong. Would I like her to point them out?

Would I like her to point them out? Was she for real? Would I like her to jump over the lane divider and hold my head underwater? Same answer.

I groaned, a guttural grimace she mistook for a yes.

For starters, my butt drooped, my head was flat, and my feet were too near the bottom of the pool. As near as I can figure it, the only things working somewhat efficiently were my floppy triceps. I must have been close to a 90-degree angle as I slugged through the water. To have her tell it, I might as well have just walked from one end of the pool to the other.

There went my Olympic dream. Unless I created a mental contest in which dragging one's bloated body through the water was an aquatic event, I would have to just stick with the shark scenario—provided I ever decided to swim laps again.

And yes, I know what my problem is. In my mind I pretend to be invincible, heroic, and brilliant. I conjure up all kinds of scenarios where I foil a plot to detonate a bomb, or rescue a blind person and her Seeing Eye dog from a burning building, win the jackpot on *Jeopardy*, or master the spinach soufflé. The trouble is, I can't live in my imagination. And even though my brain works overtime to find some place where I'm adequate, or appreciated, or, better yet, both, this is where I struggle: seeing myself as God does.

For example:

Weight

I tell myself these extra pounds I carry are no big deal. But then my friend Joanna sends a picture of me in a cowgirl outfit at her brother's 60th birthday country and western bash, and my nose looks like a third cheek. Let's not even discuss my stomach; who ever said turning sideways makes you look thinner?

Cooking

My philosophy? Presentation is overrated. My friends disagree. Why else would they suggest I make my own cookbook, one with pictures of what the dishes are *supposed* to look like on the left, and pictures of what they look like when I make them on the right? (Side note: friends are soooooo overrated.)

Gardening

If I hear "Just give it a little water when it is dry" one more time, I am going to practice my pruning skills on the nursery worker's tongue who just sold me "a plant you cannot kill." It's a racket. "Little" means what? A thimble? A full milk jug? With ambiguous terminology like that, I have no chance. Which is why my plant faithfully breaks all Guinness horticulture records for premature death. But I don't let that stop me. I'll not be beaten by something I'm supposed to outlive. Someone has to keep the nursery retail economy in the black—which, not ironically, matches my gardening thumb.

Language

When it comes to grammar, I excel. After all, I'm frequently asked to edit the writings of friends, noting their improper conjugations and misuse of pronouns. But then I go into a curriculum meeting and Mrs. Price, our senior English instructor, begins discussing descriptive writing using litotes, and I have no idea what she's talking about. (And yes, thank you much, another sentence-ending preposition.)

Fasting

Jesus fasted. In Scripture we read of the importance of fasting and praying.[48] I get that. I believe in it. I am just a colossal failure at it. The first time I attempted to get closer to God by fasting, I went to bed that night with an elephant stomping on my head. Too, the longer that day progressed, the meaner I became. No one liked me, not my husband or my kids. Probably not even God. My second attempt, liquids only, wasn't much better. Although I didn't quite hit the serial killer mode, it did not escape my notice that my kids disappeared the minute they heard my footsteps—or heard my moaning from hunger pains. My solution? Blending. Don't waste your time. There's something just plain nasty about pureed roast beef, mashed potatoes and gravy, corn on the cob, biscuits, and apple pie.

Hospitality

My friend Elaine is a crazy-talented artist. You know, the kind who creates a kitchen table out of mosaic tiles and paints historical murals for hospitals and has never met a color she doesn't like. Going to her house for dinner conjures up all sorts of feelings of inadequacy. Placemats complement napkins held together by exquisite rings she designed impromptu from leftover egg cartons, dandelions, and shoestrings. By the time she adds her innovative magic, they could be found at every Realtor's home showing and would sell for fifty dollars each at Pottery Barn.

I, on the other hand, consider it most clever to host dinner parties with a "create your own placemat" concept. Construction paper, colored pencils, glitter, and glue are mainstays for my get-togethers.

Directions

I have struggled to overcome all of the above, but the helplessness I feel when it comes to directions is overwhelming. For years, Dave—whose brain, by the way, is hardwired to an intrinsic GPS—thought I was faking it, like purporting incompetence would be scrapbook material or something. But honestly, how does one fake directions? You either get where you are going or you don't.

Even exiting hotel rooms, where there is at least a 50 percent success rate, is a challenge which I routinely fail . . . no matter how many nights I've stayed there. And driving? More frustrating than the bathroom scale. I tell Dave it's not my fault. The car GPS speaks gibberish. For example, I type in where I am going and the computer woman tells me to head south, like I know which direction that is when there are four to choose from. Why she can't simplify things by describing the gray house with the white shutters on the corner as a starting point is anyone's guess!

Dave doesn't help.

"Patty, you're going the wrong way."

"I am not. There's something at the next exit I've been dying to see."

"And what would that be?"

"It's a surprise."

The entire "Point A to Point B" tests my competence. Instead of being grateful for a husband who is equipped with a talent I am missing, I dig my heels in and become upset when my attempts to reach my destination quickly fail. I know better, for even though being inadequate (directional or otherwise) is a bummer, I never should allow those issues to color what I think of myself. Truth be told, I'm pretty sure Satan grabs his fringed horn, passes out Stogies, and celebrates every time my competition becomes other people, real or imaginary. I am a fool when I give him that power.

> **I'm pretty sure Satan grabs his fringed horn, passes out Stogies, and celebrates every time my competition becomes other people, real or imaginary. I am a fool when I give him that power.**

Not to mention, I'm not pleasing my Savior.

So why do I continue to do what I know is immature and envious and self-serving?

Since Dave and I retired, we spend our winters in Mazatlán, Mexico. For the most part, I stay indoors or in the shade because, when I was a teenager, I put Crisco on my skin and laid on the roof until my skin peeled, my freckles all blended, and now, years later, I am a poster child for skin cancer. Because of that, the sun is not my amiga and my dermatologist stays in business.

And yes, I am happy that your smooth, olive skin is blemish-free and that you turn the color of a tree trunk after only 10 minutes in the sun. (It's fun to see you on Facebook.) I digress. Anyway, enough about you.

When our friends visit us in Mazatlán, we frequent several shopping places that keep my girlfriends happy and the Mexico economy thriving. One of my friends, Pam, visits yearly with her husband, and since shopping is her favorite activity, we spend much of our time in malls or stores that sell silver at discount prices.

Pam and I met in the early '80s when her husband, Scott, was a pitcher for the New York Yankees' AAA team in Columbus, Ohio, and Dave, my husband, was the team's pitching coach. We were both raising young, neurotic boys who all loved baseball, and since we lived in the same apartment complex, we hung out together.

About Pam. She is striking—a definite head-turner. And talented. She sings (has a CD to prove it), acts (some commercials and a bit part in *Dumb and Dumber*), paints (Google "Pamela Nielsen" and check out her work), and dances (competitively). All things I dream of doing, but hey, I would rather use my talents on other things—you know, like plucking chin hairs and shaving my big toes.

If you happen to be the least bit unconfident, Pam should not be your shopping chum. She will find the five-dollar secondhand bargain outfit that gets a kajillion more compliments than the $150 one you saved for over a year to buy. More frustrating than that is how Pam's chic outfits are found for such cheap prices, especially to someone not me.

The point is, no matter what Pam wears, people bump into lampposts and each other ogling her. Possibly because they, like me, have no idea what it's like to wear a belt with no inner tube of fat cascading over the top of it, fat that not even Spandex can squash down into the thighs. And while we're on the subject of Spandex . . . did you know that chiffon pants can fall off of you at your son's wedding because of how slick that material is? Trust me on this one.

Anyway, the last time we shopped, Pam tried on a jacket. As fast as you can say "Raise your hand if you hate Pam," women surrounded her wanting to know on what rack she found her deal. When I pointed out that she was drawing a crowd of admirers, Pam told me I was being silly. So, to make a point, I tried on the same jacket . . . well, not the *same* jacket, because Pam is half my size, but you get what I'm writing. Not only did I put it on, I walked the entire store, aisle after aisle, giving anyone who was interested in looking stunning an opportunity to question this find . . . only no one even acknowledged me, except to give me a dirty look when I ran into their cart.

A few minutes later, Pam tried on a pair of shoes. Same song, different tap dance.

Nauseating. What started out as merely annoying turned into me wanting to tie myself to railroad tracks.

Here we were, a few years later. Perfect Pam and I walked into a jewelry store in Mazatlán's Golden Zone, only to be greeted by saleslady Jessie who stared intently at Pam like she was Lady Gaga or something. Typical for the employees there, Jessie spoke proficient English, and as she eyeballed Pam, her adulation escalated. Sooooo weird. Using her cupped hands to form a large parenthesis shape, outlining P.P.'s face, she began: "You . . . you have such an aura about you. Yes, yes, it's an aura. Oh my. You have such peace and beauty. Oh, this is rare indeed."

I glanced at my friend, who feigned embarrassment by the freaky attention. Then I turned to Jessie. Jessie, who would be robbed blind if any potential thief entered her store. Jessie, who was about to enter a coma from which she might never wake up. Jessie, who had no idea I was gawking at her because she could not stop gawking at P.P.

I cleared my throat.

No results.

I interrupted, feigning interest in a silver bracelet. Jessie was forced to look my direction. I somehow had managed to divert her attention from her idol.

"What about me?" I asked.

Jessie gave me the once-over. "Uh . . ." Pause, pause, pause, pause, pause. ". . . no." Then, returning her gaze to Pam, she said, "But your friend, she is magnificent." To this day, we both explode with laughter when I bring it up. Sort of like this:

Ha-ha-ha-ha-ha.

See, I laugh.

Fast forward to the mall where Pam and I were trying to figure out clothing sizes. Some sweet young thing sensed our confusion and came over to ask if we needed help. Pam asked what size she should look for. Without hesitation, the worker said, "chico." When it was my turn, I was told "grande."

Little Ms. Smarty Mouth wasn't fooling around. My side of the store, where dresses doubled as RV covers, had oversized tags with "G" denoting the size. Such an ugly word, don't you agree? *Grande!* Like *gross.* Or *gigundous.* Or *gargantuan. Giraffe. Glaucoma. Grease. Guacamole.* (Which, the last one, muchas gracias, I can eat my body weight in in a single serving, given a chance.)

> Pam asked what size she should look for. Without hesitation, the worker said, "chico." When it was my turn, I was told "grande."

Then I remind myself there's no significant difference between a chico and a grande—except, of course, a "medio," which falls somewhere between the two. Nothing except about one thousand calories a day versus five thousand, or zippers versus elastic, or an all-you-can-eat super-sized buffet versus a whiff of lettuce.

For the rest of the afternoon I could not shake how I had been described. "*Grande!* You're a chico, Pam. I'm a *grande.*" Perfect Pam thought this hysterical.

I needed another friend.

An XXG one.

I imagine Theodore Roosevelt had the likes of me in mind when he said, "Comparison is the thief of joy." I was joyless all right. In fact, I was consumed by joylessness. I took the "joy" out of "lessness." I was a "lessness."

Later, when I try to elicit concern from my not-so-empathetic husband by sharing how humiliated I was, he said he didn't understand how I could be so sensitive when the poor sales clerk was just trying to be truthful. Then he accused me of making it into a big deal. "Patty, I'm sure she didn't say it with the emphasis you're putting on it. You're yelling 'grande.' That's what makes it sound bad."

"Dave," I press, "there's no way grande can sound dainty. Pam is a chico. I'm a grande. My day is ruined. I'm going to bed."

This incident was minimized a year later in Mazatlán when another girlfriend asked her size and was told "whopper." Not XG. *Whopper!*

Without the extra-large order of fries, I guess.

Which made me momentarily stop eating my Haagen Dazs and think, *Maybe* grande *isn't so bad after all.*

It really is in the mouth of the beholder.

So, let's make a pact. From now on, you and I will be real. Special at some things, not so special at others, and maybe even pretty terrible at others. Let's permit God to give different gifts to different people and be happy about it.

Deal?

Deal.

And now, if you will excuse me, I've collected some leftover egg cartons, dandelions, and shoestrings.

I plan to create a door wreath.

Check Pottery Barn, if you're interested.

twenty-three

WHEN THE NEEDLE
SAYS 'EMPTY'

Be different. There are many more pretty
women than there are joyful ones.

ANONYMOUS

We tap-dance faster and faster, sacrificing, hoping someone will notice. We are desperate for self-worth, and the search for it is paramount in why and how we do things. We dig in our heels and take risks where we are assured success, but we run for cover if there is the slightest potential for failure.

God grieves that we concern ourselves with (i.e., fear) what others think of us. What a waste of a moment, an hour, a day, a week, a month, a year, a decade, a life! Instead of focusing on how precious we are to our loving Father, we yield to others who

239

also are wasting their days, weeks, months, years, decades, and lives doing the same. We of "sound mind" must ask ourselves just how sound our minds are if we *choose* to buy into the negative opinions of others, if we give someone else the right to define us instead of stopping long enough to ask ourselves three questions:

1. Does this person love me unconditionally?

2. Does this person have my best interests at heart?

3. What does this person stand to gain by trying to make me feel bad about myself?

Jesus, our ultimate example, knew the difference. A couple of Bible verses make my point. Luke 4:15 tells us Jesus was teaching in the synagogue, receiving praise from all the worshipers. Fair enough. John 2:23-25 explains what the Messiah thought of their praises. *Now while he was in Jerusalem at the Passover Festival, many people saw the signs he was performing and believed in his name. But Jesus would not entrust himself to them, for he knew all people. He did not need any testimony about mankind, for he knew what was in each person.*

Jesus refused to buy into the crowd's accolades because he knew they were fickle. One has only to look at the crucifixion and wonder where all his praisers were as he hung, bleeding on a cross, paying for their sins (and ours) and praying for their souls (and ours). Except for John and a few brave women, not even his band of disciples hung around. Gracious sakes alive, they stuffed their togas into their roped waistbands and skedaddled on out of there without looking back.

Still, Jesus would not allow the phoniness of the crowd's faithfulness to prevent him from doing what his Father needed him to do on the cross. Praising him or despising him, it mattered not. If Jesus didn't care what others thought of him, what keeps us from doing likewise?

In Francis Chan's *Letters to the Church*, he shares a poignant message: "One of the biggest mistakes we make is to allow proud people to consume our thoughts. We allow our minds to replay the instances when others have offended us. This robs us of our joy and robs God of the worship He deserves."[49]

When my husband coached, he had a poster on the wall in his office. It read:

> *Watch your thoughts; they become your words.*
> *Watch your words; they become your actions.*
> *Watch your actions; they become your habits.*
> *Watch your habits; they become your character.*
> *Watch your character; it becomes your destiny.*

Our brains are magnets. If we think blessings, we will attract blessings. If we think *problems*, we will attract problems. Someone sent me an email with these words: "Today somebody called me pretty. Well, actually, they called me 'pretty obnoxious,' but I choose to focus only on the positives." You've got to love it!

The way we think controls our destiny. Need proof?

Romans 12:2

Do not copy the behavior and customs of this world, but let God transform you into a new person by changing the way you think. Then you will learn to know God's will for you, which is good and pleasing and perfect

2 Corinthians 10:5

We demolish arguments and every pretension that sets itself up against the knowledge of God, and we take captive every thought to make it obedient to Christ.

Philippians 4:8

Whatever is noble, whatever is right, whatever is pure, whatever is lovely, whatever is admirable—if anything is excellent or praiseworthy—think about such things.

Proverbs 23:7

As someone thinks within himself, so he is.

Those verses are not debatable; we are to think Christlike thoughts. Why? Because positive self-talk will transform us into a new creation. Negative self-talk, conversely, has the potential to keep us frozen and unwilling to move forward. Not to mention, believing we are losers! And the more we allow that negative self-talk to take hold, those "I'm so homely" or "What an idiot I am!" or "Everyone has it so much better than I do" thoughts become our reality. A reality that takes root and dictates our future, a future that is the antithesis of what God wants for us.

The Vincent Van Gogh exhibit was in Sarasota, Florida, and my daughter-in-law Kristen bought tickets for us to attend. The genius artist lived a tormented life, and I was sad to read his quotes displayed on temporary walls. "What am I in the eyes of most people? A non-entity or an oddity or a disagreeable person—someone who has, and will have no position in society, in short a little lower than the lowest. Very well—assuming that everything is indeed like that, then through my work I'd like to show what there is in the heart of such an oddity, such a nobody."[50]

Contrast that with the confidence of Picasso, who said this: "When I was a child my mother said to me, 'If you become a soldier, you'll be a general. If you become a monk, you'll be the pope.' Instead, I became a painter and wound up as Picasso."

Recently I spent time with my sweet friend, author Lael Arrington. I asked if she remembered times when she felt inadequate. She pulled up a post from her high school journal. After being crowned "Miss Beautiful," this is what she wrote: *"But as the night of the beauty pag-*

eant wore on, a curious thing happened. The applause drained away. There I was at the very pinnacle of my high school dreams, watching my best friend and [the] runner-up, Judy, leave with her boyfriend. My boyfriend and I had parted company, and so I left with my parents for ice cream at my uncle's house. I heard Peggy Lee's song even though the stereo wasn't on. 'Is that all there is? Is that all there is?' Being chosen and even crowned somehow wasn't enough. The needle on my heart-tank fell to empty."

Sadly, far too often most of us allow our needles to fall to empty. Even more damaging is how we are wired to keep them there. We obsess over the negatives. Researchers say it takes seven positive comments to undo one negative comment.[51] I'm not sure it doesn't take more. At this point in writing this book, I am 72 years old. I have had my share of compliments, and I know that I am deeply loved by God, but (and I'm not proud to admit this) I seem to be able to recall with much greater clarity the negatives that called my adequacy into question.

- The lady who publicly attacked my Christian talk because I spoke of our youngest son spending time in the burn unit following a bonfire accident. (Her son had died—which must have been horrific—so what did I know about pain?)

- The joke that bombed when I said my favorite color was "school bus yellow" because my kids would be out of my hair, not knowing that my audience was made up of homeschooling mothers. (Soooooo not my fault. Beth Moore told it and all three thousand people at her talk roared with laughter.)

- A friendship lost over a misunderstood text.

When I dwell on what God thinks of me, none of those negatives will be given the undue attention I might offer them. As John Burke puts it in his book *Imagine Heaven,* "God never created us to get our identity from what we do or what others did to us, but from who we are to God."[52] Once God becomes the One in which we delight, we will begin to recognize His purpose in creating us. We *must* replace our thoughts about who we are with God's thoughts about the same.

Later in the Van Gogh exhibit, the artist's despair (and eventual suicide) became obvious when I read that after his failures led to him becoming an artist, he said this (in September 1888): "In life and in painting too, I can easily do without the dear Lord, but I can't, suffering as I do, do without something greater than myself, which is my life, the power to create."[53]

Buying into what God says about me (*I am a child of God*—John 1:12; *I am a new creation*—2 Corinthians 5:17; *I am a victor*—Romans 8:37; *I am designed for good works*—Ephesians 2:10), each day is a fresh opportunity to radiate light and not darkness. We all should have that message posted on our mirrors to remind us of how amazing we really are. Light will cause me to turn off that nasty recording reminding me of all the times I haven't lived up to the expectations of others. If I allow my tape loop of embarrassments or putdowns to run, I will be picking dusty bunnies under my bed, a picture of total crazy!

I simply refuse to allow a few hundred screwups to determine my self-worth. Are you "Amen, Sister"ing me here?

I mean, so what if I arrived at work with the back of my skirt tucked into my underwear?

So what if my husband attempted to bolster my self-confidence by saying that he never would want to be married to a young, skinny person?

So what if I ran into an old friend and told her I had never seen her hair look so flattering . . . and she told me it was a wig because she was battling cancer?

So what if I got a little too excited when I ran into Reggie Jackson?

Let me explain.

My stepdaughter Nikki, her daughter, Amanda, and I were in New York City celebrating my granddaughter's recent high school graduation when we walked out of our hotel and I spotted Reggie Jackson, a famous retired baseball player who once played on the same team as my husband. He was visiting with a group of friends, waiting for a cab. Dave had run into him a few years back, and they had a nice visit. Nikki and Amanda encouraged me to introduce myself (and them). Getting up the nerve, I neared where he was standing and waited for a pause in his conversation.

"Mr. Jackson?" I began.

"Yes," he responded, turning from his friends. *Sweet. He didn't motion for his bodyguards.*

"I'm Patty LaRoche. My husband Dave played on the Yankees with you in the '80s."

He nodded, still smiling, but said nothing . . . nothing. No matter how many facts I added to refresh his memory.

"He was a reliever . . .

"It was several years ago . . .

"You were both on the same team . . .

"The Yankees . . .

"A long time ago . . .

"Around '80-'83 . . .

"Dave LaRoche is his name . . .

"He was left-handed . . .

"You both were in the World Series together . . .

"His last year there was 1983 . . .

"You ran into him a short while back and had a nice conversation . . ."

This was ridiculous! How dare he not remember my husband! Pitiful! The two of them were on the same field together, traveled together, spent time in the trainer's room together, ate together. Did I need to show him an 8x10 glossy? Rivulets of sweat streamed from my armpits.

Or perhaps this was a joke. Reggie Jackson was messing with me. Any second now he would say, "Just kidding. Of course I remember Dave. What a great pitcher and a great guy he was!"

Absolutely he would say that.

Finally, Mr. Hoity-Toity Jackson opened his mouth.

"Uh, Ma'am," he said. "I'm not Reggie Jackson. I'm Jessie Jackson."

I would die friendless.

There isn't adequate space here to list all the bumbling words I stuttered while looking for a New York sewer hole to fall into while trying to preserve a modicum of what itsy bitsy dignity I had left. My family—whom I was desperately trying to impress—was no support. Apologizing profusely as I backed away, I found them behind a pillar, holding their stomachs, tears leaving cascades of eyeliner streaming down their cheeks.

Dave didn't find it funny when I phoned him to tell him what happened. "You did what? Patty, they look nothing alike."

"Well, how in the world was I supposed to know that?"

But the more I dwelled on it—which was the majority of the hours left in that day, thanks to Nikki and Amanda—the more I realized I probably had made Mr. Jackson's day. Yeah. I was certain of it. Who wouldn't want to be likened to a Hall of Fame baseball player? It was the ultimate compliment. And the next time we run into each other, I plan to tell him that. But in case we never do . . .

You are most welcome, Mr. Jackson!

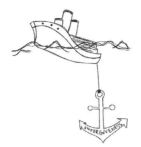

twenty-four

TAKE AWAY THE ENEMY'S POWER: FORGIVE

When you forgive, you in no way change the past—
but you sure do change the future.
Bernard Meltzer

The word *forgive* is found 127 times in the Bible. There's no way to misinterpret how important it is. We. Must. Forgive. In Luke 6:37 Jesus explains its seriousness: *"Judge not, and you will not be judged; condemn not, and you will not be condemned; forgive, and you will be forgiven."* Stop right there. No matter what has happened to you, Jesus tells us that we won't be forgiven if we don't figure out a way to forgive.

Brooke Axtell is the daughter of my good friend Mollie. Our families were members of the same church when we lived in Texas. Cal, Brooke's father, and Mollie led a Bible study in which Dave and I were involved. Our three sons and their three children would hang out when we all were together. When Brooke was a teenager, she told her parents that she had been sex-trafficked by their Christian nanny when she was seven. Her book, *Beautiful Justice: Reclaiming My Worth After Human Trafficking and Sexual Abuse,* tells the story of her horrific experience and redemption. She knows well what it is like to have others make her feel unloved. She wrote:

> "We have all been lied to about who we are. Through trauma, relationships, and media, we have been taught that we are not good enough. We are bombarded by the message that we are separated from the love we crave and seduced into believing that if we strive harder, accomplish more, give more, perform our roles, buy new products, follow new gurus, or subject ourselves to another diet of self-help program, we will finally arrive.

> "But the glimpses of joy and peace do not last because they are built on the underlying fallacy that we have to earn love and prove our worth by changing our external circumstances.

> "You may be in pain right now. You may feel disconnected from the truth of your unconditional worth. But nothing can take away your value.

> "There is nothing you can do to make God love you any less. And there is nothing you can do to make God love you any more. This is the way of wild grace. It is safe to rest here."[54]

To be the blessing God wants us to be, we have to do what I believe can be torturously difficult. We have to forgive. Hundreds of books have been written on the subject. Hundreds of powerful clichés address it. But I wanted the girls in my living room to focus on the type of forgiveness required when we've been rejected or made to feel inadequate.

I know people like Brooke whose journeys have required a level of forgiveness I cannot imagine.

- "Gretchen" was a victim of satanic, ritual abuse when she was a child. Through years of therapy, she has accepted that the "Jesus" fakes who molested her did not represent the true Savior who loves her unconditionally.

Forgiveness.

- Debbie Parnham, an amazing lady I met at a speaking engagement in Arizona, led her son's murderer to Christ and defended him at his parole hearing after he randomly chose her son as his target in a drive-by shooting.

Forgiveness.

- "Brenda" refused to allow a pastor's words to continue wounding her when, after her teenager died in a car wreck, she was told her son would not be in Heaven because he never was baptized.

Forgiveness.

- Barbara was told daily by her mother that she was a "stupid idiot," and she was beaten so regularly by her father, a policeman, that the gym teacher allowed her to not wear the usual gym clothes so she would not reveal her bruises. Today, Barbara is 59 and, when asked where her confidence comes from, she says "God. He's always been with me."

Forgiveness.

- My husband was 27 when he received a letter from his biological father who had not had contact with him for twenty-one years. Dave answered his request for baseball equipment for the three half-brothers he had never met.

Forgiveness.

Definition: what *I* did not have toward Dave's father. Dave never received a birthday card, a Christmas phone call, not even a congratulations when he signed a professional baseball contract. He taught himself to play baseball by throwing a ball against his backyard wall instead of playing catch with his dad, like his friends did with theirs. And now he was asked to send his father's three teenage sons some baseball equipment? You know, the sons his father was supporting and living with and loving? The things he never did with my husband, his firstborn son?

After my tirade (which continued well after Dave boxed up some baseball gear), my husband reminded me that he refused to give anyone the power to make him feel less about himself than God intended.

He understood forgiveness. He understood moving on. He understood the trap set for him by Satan should he choose to live in bitterness. He understood that forgiveness is about his attitude, not the other person's actions.

> He understood forgiveness. He understood moving on. He understood the trap set for him by Satan should he choose to live in bitterness.

Should we harbor unforgiveness, we are sinking ships. Peace eludes us, and we become slaves to bitterness, which ensnares us, causing us, most importantly, to lose joy.

The girls in my living room needed to forgive: one, a parent, for deserting her and being too busy to be part of her life; another, a boyfriend for using her for sex and then leaving her for another virgin; another, classmates who mocked her cheerleading tryout. Every girl curled up on my couches had a story. Some more than one.

So when I told them they needed to repent for their part in the abuse, they were shocked. It turned out to be one of the best Bible studies we had. They began sharing about resentments they had toward their offenders. About how they had grieved God by not believing how He viewed them but had, instead, given so much power to their "enemies," and realizing that simply calling the perpetrators "enemies" was a grievance against what Jesus required. How choices they had made not to recognize that God could use these situations to bless them or grow them into better Christians required repentance.

I told the girls to turn to Hebrews 8:12: *"For I will be merciful to their unrighteousness, and their sins and their lawless deeds I will remember no more."* God was doing His part. Now the teens needed to do theirs. We looked at Isaiah 43:18, 19 (from The Message): *Forget about what's happened; don't keep going over old history. Be alert, be present. I'm about to do something brand-new. It's bursting out! Don't you see it?*

🏆   🏆   🏆

Any time we allow someone else to dictate our value, our adequacy, our self-worth, we are allowing their view of us to trump God's. For that we need to ask His forgiveness.

If you're like me, forgiveness is hard. The wounds are deep, and they continue to fester. But if we are to grow in our faith, if we are to be living disciples of a mighty God, if we are to exude joy, we must— *must!*—ask God to teach us to forgive.

When I was 26 and into my sixth month of pregnancy, I began bleeding. Two previous pregnancies had ended in miscarriage, so I knew the warning signs. My husband was on the Cleveland Indians baseball team, and the families had been invited on a road trip to California, where a day at Disneyland was included. Dave and I were there when I told him I needed to get to a hospital.

As it turned out, the hospital emergency room personnel were more impressed with meeting Dave than attending to me. He, a former California Angels pitcher, had just been selected for that year's All-Star team, and he had been featured in area newspapers. Getting an autograph from him made their day.

I was admitted to the hospital and Dave was told I would be fine; he could go ahead with his team to play against Oakland. Convinced that I was in good hands, Dave boarded the team plane. When the doctor came to my room, he kept saying that I was in my eighth month of pregnancy, refusing to believe me when I told him he was wrong.

A routine exam was anything but; the doctor broke my water, putting me into premature labor.

Our tiny baby boy lived three hours.

The following morning, flowers were delivered to my room—a gift from this doctor, who had to be terrified of a malpractice lawsuit. It is an understatement to say that I have never been sadder. I entered a very dark time in my life.

Forgiveness was not on my radar.

I did not share that story with the teens in my living room because this was about them, not me. I share it here to let you know that I could empathize with these gals and understood how difficult it can be to forgive. The breakthrough at our Bible study that night was indescribable, each girl taking time to ask forgiveness for her part in the actions that left her scarred. An immense healing had happened in their lives, and none of us were tearless when the evening was over.

My prayer for you is that you refuse to refuse to forgive. Let's revisit Luke 6:37: *"Do not judge, and you will not be judged. Do not condemn, and you will not be condemned. Forgive, and you will be forgiven."* This passage makes it clear that no one benefits more when we release others from our ugly, vengeful thoughts than we do. Scripture lets us know that this is for our own, eternal well-being.

Its importance cannot be understated. Jesus' last words while hanging on the cross should never be dismissed: "It is finished."[55] He paid the price. He chose forgiveness. We, in our sinful state, were worth His very life. Should we consider our judgments of others who have wounded us more valid than His?

If we hold on to the pain caused by someone else, we suffer. By forgiving the offense, we free ourselves from living in the bitterness which will suffocate us and cause us to become joyless. Not the way God wants us to live.

The most difficult part of forgiveness is to truly release our offender into God's care. There are always reminders of how we were wounded, and if we engage in "faux forgiveness," we will find ourselves dragged back into joylessness. One author said it well: "We put our resentments in cold storage and then pull the switch to let them thaw out again. Our grudges are taken out of the lake of prayer to drown them, and we end up giving them a swimming lesson. How often have we torn up the canceled note, but hang on to the wastebasket that holds the pieces? This is not to say that human forgiveness does not occur, only that it is rare and that much that passes for forgiveness is often not so at all."[56]

Lord, let me not be guilty of such.

I've thought a lot about this. To *not* forgive is selfish. It holds to the standard that I am more valued than my offender, that I am somehow entitled to always be treated with dignity and respect and never with less regard than the incredibly entitled, special person I am. It refuses to allow God to work through me so I can grow in my faith-walk and dependence on Him. It shoves God off His throne and puts me in charge. It is all God is not. His forgiveness toward His children has no limits. Neither should ours.

A.W. Tozer reminds us of what God is up to when we go through hurtful times. "When I understand that everything happening to me is to make me more Christlike," the great pastor and author wrote, "it resolves a great deal of anxiety."[57]

> I struggled looking at babies in strollers or talking about friends' pregnancies. And I hated what I was becoming.

Following our baby's death, I plunged into a pit of darkness. Why would God allow this—and for the third time? What if I never could have children? When I was invited to a baby shower for a wife on the team, I made up an excuse why I couldn't go. I struggled looking at babies in strollers or talking about friends' pregnancies. And I hated what I was becoming.

Eileen, a friend from the Catholic church I attended at the time, was worried about me. She pestered me to attend an evangelistic outreach led by a Baptist pastor, but since the event wasn't Catholic, I told her I wasn't interested. Eileen reminded me that she was Catholic but had heard this pastor before and knew I would be blessed. Finally, to get her off my back, I told her I would go but would sit in the back of the church and not listen to anything he said.

Yes, I know, a terrible attitude. I chose a seat on the back pew, folded my arms, and scowled. But when the altar call came, God got my attention. I ran to the front of the church, knelt on the altar, and sobbed into the arms of some poor man who had to question if he was entering a faith of crazies.

I asked God to forgive my faithlessness, for only wanting Him when He gave me what I thought I needed. I began reading the Bible, joined Bible studies, and ultimately became a member of a nondenominational church. My life has never been the same.

I once read that we don't forgive people because we are weak; we forgive them because we are strong enough to know that people make mistakes. It is not forgetting or putting on spiritual airs like something painful did not happen. Many times it is an ongoing process that takes time. It does not mean that we now need to seek a restored relationship. It simply means that we will not allow ourselves to dwell on our pain. In many cases it requires us to ask God to forgive through us. After all, His ability to forgive is limitless, and He loves when we call on Him to meet that need.

So when those memories return, instead of inviting them to take root, instead of getting a buzz from hearing that something bad has happened to our offender, the only thing we need to say is, "Thank you, God, for reminding me of the power to forgive."

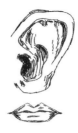

twenty-five

SO, WHAT'S A PERSON TO DO?

Our time is limited, so don't waste it living someone else's life.
STEVE JOBS

One of the most energizing ways to be beautiful is to invest your time in others. Learn to ask questions and listen well. Most people love to tell their stories but have few opportunities to do so, and if you learn to be captivated by what they tell you, they feel valued. In reality, you help them love themselves just a little more than before your conversation started. Which, not surprisingly, gives *you* value in *their* eyes. And probably even in your own.

When I taught high school speech, every year on day one I used the same drill. Students were randomly paired and told to face each other just 18 inches apart. Partner A was to ask questions of Partner B for two minutes with the objective of building upon what he or she had just heard. Then the sides were reversed. My first few years this was not a difficult assignment, but the more cellphones became the teens' number one source of communication (don't get me started!), the more paralyzing the assignment seemed to be. Most students were out of questions after fifteen seconds and stared at me to throw them a verbal lifeline.

The exercise was frustrating, and the more I analyzed what I was witnessing, the sadder I became. How many friendships would they deny themselves because they had no idea how to engage a stranger? Was that the reason so many of our students lasted only a semester when they went away to college and then had to return to our small town—because that was familiar territory? What a loss for them to never appreciate what they could glean from someone of another culture or race or socioeconomic status or gender!

I hope you are one who will risk asking questions. More importantly, I hope you learn to listen well. Years ago I flew to Florida to see my husband and two of our sons; all three were in the middle of baseball's spring training. It was an early morning flight, and going on three hours of sleep is never fun, so I was grateful to find an available window seat where I could rest my head and catch up on some slumber.

A couple entering the cabin after me opted for the aisle seats, she in my row and her husband across from her. Behind them came another couple. Realizing there were no two seats left that were together, I offered to give one of them my seat so they wouldn't be separated. The wife rejected my overture and took the middle seat directly in front of her husband who sat between me and the woman in the aisle seat. Immediately the two in my row began talking . . . and talking . . . and talking.

For the entire two-plus hours they rarely came up for air. Had I croaked, they wouldn't have noticed. Covering about every subject imaginable, they switched gears like a NASCAR driver. From their travel plans to their children to their love of lasagna to their religion to the problems with catheters used on them during their hospital stays (I'm not making this up), they became so familiar with each other that they actually exchanged e-mail addresses when they deplaned. Occasionally they would attempt to converse with their own spouses through the seats or across the aisle: "Hey, Bob, Mike here just bought a truck too." "Sue, you're not going to believe this, but Donna likes granite countertops just like you do." When their mates grunted or failed to reply, my aisle-mates seemed nonplussed and continued on with their own verbal ping-pong.

But there was something else. "Donna" never allowed "Mike" to complete a story. She was the poster child for the classic interruption. Mike started to discuss how he had confronted his "hillbilly neighbors about the weed their son was hiding on his truck's front tire," but as soon as he took a breath, she started her saga about her neighbor who had actually caused her best friend to leave the neighborhood. The man didn't finish one story; trust me, this was very frustrating. It was all I could do not to ask Donna to "just zip it!" so I could find out how Mike's neighbor responded to his tattling.

In the high school speech textbook I used, Donna's mode of communicating is referred to as self-centered listening. We listen *only* to think of what we're going to say next. I know it well; it's the type of listening I do far too frequently when I'm conversing with God. Dumping my "to-do list" in His lap without asking Him to help me set priorities . . . allowing my mind to wander during my quiet time . . . reading the Bible and wondering why friends and family members don't do what it says . . . disregarding what my conscience tells me to do when the alternative is so much more fun . . . not recognizing His many blessings in the course of a day. These are all methods I've used.

How many times is God trying to get my attention but I'm too focused on what I want to say? And how much am I missing because I am too self-absorbed to listen for His instruction and inspiration leading me to a closer walk with Him? "Listening" to the conversation on that flight reminded me of how much I need to "zip it!" and give God a chance.

In the scheme of things, it really doesn't matter if Donna listened to Mike on that flight. But the repercussions of me not listening to my Heavenly Father are much more critical. Donna only ran the risk of losing the opportunity to learn something about—or from—Mike. Compare that to the loss of opportunity to learn something about or from God. A life of faith is a life grounded in communion with God, and it is no coincidence that the root of the English word communion is the same as for the word "communication."

If we desire to have healthy communication with one another, it's important to remember that we need to listen as well as speak. And when it comes to communication, and thus communion, with God, aren't we being a little arrogant if we fail to recognize that listening is the most important part?

> When we show a genuine interest in others, when we care enough to join in their story, we let them know they matter. We are confirming the message God wants us all to have: *we are valued.*

When we show a genuine interest in others, when we care enough to join in their story, we let them know they matter. We are confirming the message God wants us all to have: *we are valued.*

In the nursing home where my mother was a resident, a wonderful woman named Judy, the social director, constantly came up with ways to engage the elderly who lived there. One day she encouraged them to tell something about themselves that no one else knew. A somber eighty-six-year-old man began talking about how his parents had placed him for adoption when he was five years old. They kept his sibling but could not afford both sons. In the middle of his story, the elderly gentleman broke down sobbing. All those years he had clung to his sadness and refused to share his pain. I had to wonder: *Before Judy, did anyone ever care to ask?*

Recently I had lunch with Juliette (of eyebrow fame, Chapter 12) who told me that when she lived outside Boston, she began a hospice care for veterans. Volunteers were linked with dying veterans who had no family or friends. Juliette's first encounter was with a man who opened up as soon as he learned she spoke his German language. When she questioned his friendships, he shared that he had lost touch with his only friend, who lived in Germany. That was all it took for Juliette to find the man on Whatsapp, text him to see if he was available to talk, and reconnect the two friends.

I asked Juliette why no one in that veterans' facility had taken the time to hear his story and make that call. She had no idea. She only knew that she was as blessed as the dying man.

If you have stayed with me through this book, you know the ball is now in your court. We get one chance (literally) at this thing called life. Should you opt not to put yourself out there as a means of valuing others simply because you fear rejection or that you may run out of things to say, you are missing out on growing and learning and blossoming into what God desires for you. He wants what is best for you. He loves you unconditionally. Period. No, make that an exclamation mark. God loves you *unconditionally*!

In Max Lucado's book *When Christ Comes: The Beginning of the Very Best*, he reminds us of the day when we will know our true worth, when "What the world has overlooked, your Father has remembered . . . The day Christ comes will be a day of reward. Those who went unknown on earth will be known in Heaven. Those who never heard the cheers of men will hear the cheers of angels. Those who missed the blessing of a father will hear the blessing of their heavenly Father. The small will be great. The forgotten will be remembered. The unnoticed will be crowned and the faithful will be honored."[58]

Your day is coming. What the world has overlooked, your Father has remembered. I pray that, as you evaluate your next steps, choosing a life of joy and not fear, every thought you have will be filtered through God's yearning for your well-being. When those bouts of insecurity or those opportunities for unforgiveness or those envious emotions start to slither in, you will recognize their source and immediately substitute Christ-centered truths in their place. You will remind yourself that you are loved, valued, and precious to your Creator, who gave you gifts that need to be developed no matter how many times you mess up trying. And hopefully, yes hopefully, you will learn to laugh in the process.

Endnotes

Chapter 2: Puberty, Meet Put-downs

1. Poehler, Amy, *Yes, Please* (Dey Street Books, 2014).
2. Matthew 21:12, 13 (NIV):

> Jesus entered the temple courts and drove out all who were buying and selling there. He overturned the tables of the money changers and the benches of those selling doves. "It is written," he said to them, "'My house will be called a house of prayer,' but you are making it 'a den of robbers.'"

Chapter 3: Judging the Judge

3. Isaiah 64:8 (NIV):

> Yet you, Lord, are our Father. We are the clay, you are the potter; we are all the work of your hand.

4. Prinstein, Mitch, *Popular: The Power of Likeability in a Status-Obsessed World*. Reprinted by arrangement with Viking, an imprint of Penguin Random House LLC (2017).

Chapter 5: Will the Good Samaritan Please Stand Up?

5. Lil Phoenix, "Things God Won't Ask on That Day," www.poemhunter.com/lil-phoenix/ebooks/.
6. Lewis, C.S., *A Grief Observed* (Harper Collins, 1961).
7. Kidder, Virelle, *Meet Me at the Well* (Moody Publishers, 2008), p. 30.
8. "Mother Teresa: *Come Be My Light: The Private Writings of the Saint of Calcutta*, Kolodiejchuk, Brian, ed. (Doubleday, 2007).

Chapter 6: A Lesson from the Academy Awards

9. Tozer, A.W., *The Pursuit of God* (Gutenberg Press, 2008).

Chapter 8: A Waste of Taste

10. Martin, J.A., Hamilton, B. E., Osterman, M. J. K, and Driscoll, A. K. "Births: Final Data for 2019. Volume 70, Number 2" (Hyattsville, MD: National Center for Health Statistics, 2021). https://www.cdc.gov/nchs/data/nvsr70/nvsr70-02-508.pdf

11. *2021 National Fatherhood Initiative,* "The Statistics Don't Lie: Fathers Matter," Philadelphia, Pennsylvania.

12. Eldredge, Stasi, *Captivating: Unveiling the Mystery of a Woman's Soul* (Thomas Nelson, 2011), pp. 6, 7.

13. Philippians 1:6, NIV

Chapter 10: First, Last . . . Last, First

14. Chan, Francis, *Letters to the Church* (David C. Cook Publishing, 2018), p. 87

15. Idleman, Kyle, *The End of Me: Where Real Life in the Upside-Down Ways of Jesus Begins* (David C. Cook Distribution, 2015), p. 95.

Chapter 11: Sew What?

16. Romans 11:5.

17. Lamott, Anne, Grace *(Eventually): Thoughts on Faith* (Penguin, 2008), p.63.

18. Hebrews 13:5, NKJV.

Chapter 12: The Disease to Please

19. Braiker, Harriet, *The Disease to Please* (McGraw-Hill Education, 2000).

20. McGee, Robert S., *The Search for Significance* (The Official McGee Publishing, 1984).

Chapter 13: Dishonorable Intentions

21. Acts 1:20-26

Chapter 15: At What Point?

22. Steinbeck, John, *East of Eden* (Viking Press, 1952).

23. Goff, Bob, *Everybody Always: Becoming Love in a World Full of Setbacks and Difficult People* (Thomas Nelson, 2018).

Chapter 16: Say Yes to Fear? Say No to Joy

24. Lucado, Max, *Traveling Light* (Thomas Nelson, 2006).

25. Calvin, John, *Genesis 25 Bible Commentary,* 1564.

26. Welch, Edward T., *When People Are Big and God Is Small: Overcoming Peer Pressure, Codependency, and the Fear of Man* (P&R Publishing, 1997).

27. Ibid.

Chapter 17: It's My Pity Party and I'll Cry If I Want To

28. Steinbeck, *East of Eden* (Viking Press, 1952).

Chapter 18: Maybe Looks *Can* Kill

29. Graham, Michelle, *Wanting to Be Her: Body Image Secrets Victoria Won't Tell You,* (Intervarsity Press, 2009), pp. 90, 134, 135.

30. IBIS World's Statistics, 2022.

31. Madueme, Hans, "Nip and Tuck: A Parable," *Dignitas 16*, no. 1 (2009).

32. The Nikolov Center for Plastic Surgery, 2019.

33. Warren, Rick, *The Purpose-Driven Life: What on Earth Am I Here For?* (10th ed.) (Grand Rapids, Michigan: Zondervan, 2012).

34. Crabb, Dr. Larry, *From God to You: 66 Love Letters: A Conversation with God That Invites You Into His Story* (Thomas Nelson, 2010).

35. "Healthcare Costs," 2022, CostHelper Health, "Neck Lift Costs," www.health.costhelper.com.

36. Aquinas, Thomas, "The Sin of Envy—Seven Deadly Sins," *Summa Theologiae.*

37. "FOMO Effect": "FOMO: How the Fear of Missing Out Leads to Missing Out",

Jacqueline Rifkin, Chan Cindy, and Barbara Kahn in Advances in *Consumer Research Volume 43*, eds. Kristin Diehl and Carolyn Yoon (Duluth, Minnesota: Association for Consumer Research, 2015), pp. 244-248.

Elhai, J.D., Levine, J.C., Dvorak, R.D., & Hall, B.J., "Fear of missing out, need for touch, anxiety, and depression are related to problematic smartphone use," *Computers in Human Behavior*, 63, 509–516, www.acrwebsite.org/volumes/1019794/volumes/v43/NA-43.

38. *Motivation and Emotion,* Milyavskaya, M., Saffran, M., Hope, N., & Koestner, R., "Fear of missing out: Prevalence, dynamics, and consequences of experiencing FOMO" (2018), pp. 1-13

39. Baker, Z.G., Krieger, H., & LeRoy, A. S., "Fear of missing out: Relationships with depression, mindfulness, and physical symptoms," *Translational Issues in Psychological Science,* 2 (3) (2016), p. 275.

40. Gordon, Jon. From his LinkedIn.com profile.

Chapter 19: The Worst Failure? Failing to Try

41. Federle, Tim, *Life Is Like a Musical: How to Live, Love, and Lead Like a Star* (Running Press, 2017).

Chapter 20: The Shame of Shame

42. Eldredge, John, *Waking the Dead* (Thomas Nelson, 2016).

43. Dale Carnegie's *Scrapbook: A Treasury of the Wisdom of the Ages.*

44. Chan, *Letters to the Church,* (David C. Cook Publishing, 2018), p. 193

45. Yancey, Philip, *What's So Amazing About Grace?* (Zondervan, 2002).

46. Michele Cushatt, *I Am: A 60-Day Journey to Knowing Who You Are Because of Who He Is* (Zondervan, 2017).

Chapter 21: Kindergarten Chaos

47. Graham, *Wanting to Be Her.*

Chapter 22: Goin' Down

48. Ezra 8:23; Luke 2:37; Acts 14:23.

Chapter 23: When the Needle Says 'Empty'

49. Chan, *Letters to the Church,* (David C. Cook Publishing, 2018), p. 212

50. Vincent Van Gogh, from the Van Gogh Exhibition in Sarasota, Fla. (Quote from September 1888.)

51. Life Source, "Why It Takes 7 Positives to Reverse 1 Negative" (2017).

52. Burke, John, *Imagine Heaven* (Baker Publishing, 2017), p. 70.

53. Van Gogh exhibit.

Chapter 24: Take Away the Enemy's Power: Forgive

54. Axtell, Brooke, *Beautiful Justice: Reclaiming My Worth After Human Trafficking and Sexual Abuse* (Seal Press, 2019).

55. John 19:30.

56. Hamilton, Dan, *Forgiveness* (IVP Books, 1980), p. 7.

57. Tozer, A.W., "Aiden Wilson Tozer Quotes," www.azquotes.com/author/14750-Aiden_Wilson_Tozer .

Chapter 25: So, What's a Person to Do?

58. Lucado, Max, *When Christ Comes: The Beginning of the Very Best* (Thomas Nelson, 2014).

About the Author

Patty and Dave, her husband of 50 years, met on a blind date and married in spite of warnings from her parish priest that she would go to Hell if they did (Yes, rejected by a clergy member). Because of Dave's career in professional baseball, they have lived in over 40 cities, ranging from California to New York, many of which provided anecdotes for this book.

The couple miraculously raised three rambunctious sons, unaware they suffered from Attention Deficit Disorder (A.D.D.) until they were in their twenties and playing professional baseball. Patty admits that her children's fiercely independent behavior gave her fodder for "I bet your kid never tried this" rivalries (which, not to brag, she always won). Still, their time spent in principals' offices and later in write-ups for sports' magazines, mentioning how their mother "missed" their A.D.D. diagnosis, made her question if the area of child-raising wasn't yet another in which she did not measure up.

After retiring from teaching high school speech, theater, debate and forensics, Patty split her time between Kansas and Mexico where she volunteers for local orphanages. She speaks professionally and writes a weekly religious column for three area newspapers. When not doing her favorite thing—hanging with family—Patty plays tennis and pickleball, reads, watches N.F.L. games (Go, Chiefs!), cooks and connects with friends. She enjoys thinking about exercising and losing weight and loves telling people about Jesus.

This author finds adventures in the nuttiness of life, recognizing that no matter what role she plays—wife, mother, stepmother, grandmother, great-grandmother, teacher, speaker, athlete/coach—there is no shortage of people who have managed to pin-hole her self-esteem bubble. Intentional or not. *A Little Faith Lift* includes many of those narratives and is a reminder that we all need to strive for excellence, not acceptance, because comparing ourselves to others will prevent us from living up to our God-given potential.

That doesn't have to be

A Little Faith Lift...Finding Joy Beyond Rejection was written to encourage readers to find their worth in God and not in what others think of them. Should they choose the latter, they risk remaining peaceless, joyless, falling short of the abundant life God wants them to have. This book is written for teens...and young adults...and middle-aged adults...and senior citizens. Actually, Patty's intended audience is the majority of people she meets who have memories of betrayal by teachers, coaches, family members, friends, bullies or (you fill in the blank) who used them as their personal punching bag. Her audience has a hard time understanding that hurt people hurt people, thanks to a spiritual enemy who passes out stogies any time he can manipulate their self-worth.

These individuals measure themselves against others who have the looks, talents, or personality traits they think they lack. Walking into a room full of strangers produces enough sweat to frizz their hair, and if asked to spearhead the church social, they hyperventilate. Patty gets it. She taught public speaking to high schoolers for 20 years, but when a group of senior girls asked if she would lead them in a Bible study, the message became clear: if her students could recognize from Whom their value came—challenging in a public-school setting—and not from what others thought of them, their lives forever would be changed. An organizing principle of *A Little Faith Lift* focuses on the teens in that study.

A Little Faith Lift is for all people who doubt their worth, to help them move past the pain caused by others that has left them insecure or bitter, to teach them to accept the potential humor has over rejection. Patty's objective is to convince them to take risks and refuse to give anyone or anything the power to make them less than

God desires, to know that He's the C.E.O. of the "Beauty from Ashes" business.

Because of God, Patty shares her story, stacked with raw seriousness but mostly, evidence that humor can be found in the darkest and darnedest places.

Not surprisingly, Grace has a way of making that happen.

Connect with Patty
Instagram: patty_laroche
Twitter: Patty LaRoche@PattyLaRoche
Linkedin: Patty LaRoche
Facebook: Patty LaRoche
Tedx talk: For more information on the TEDx talk, please visit www.alittlefaithlift.com.